The Elements

THE
ELEMENTS

What You *Really* Want to Know

RON MILLER

Twenty-First Century Books
Minneapolis

Dedicated to Michael Seigel

Text and illustrations copyright © 2006 by Ron Miller

Photographs courtesy of © Corbis: pp. 48 (Ted Spiegel), 70 (Colin
Garratt/Milepost 92 $\frac{1}{2}$), 73 (Gunter Marx), 80 (Lowell Georgia), 95 (CRD
Photo), 124 (Bettmann), 126; Index Stock: p. 64 (#428115a © Inga Spence);
© Jack Novak/SuperStock: p. 72 (top); U. S. Air Force/Tech. Sgt. Michael
Haggerty: p. 77 (top); © Matt Gustantino: p. 82; © Geoffrey Wheeler: p. 98
(top); © Document General Motors/Reuter R/Corbis Sygma: p. 110;
Hulton/Archive/Getty Images: p. 122

Twenty-First Century Books
A division of Lerner Publishing Group
241 First Avenue North
Minneapolis, Minnesota 55401 U.S.A.

Website address: www.lernerbooks.com

Library of Congress Cataloging-in-Publication Data
Miller, Ron.
The elements: what you *really* want to know / Ron Miller.
p. cm.
Summary: Discusses the history of the periodic table of the elements, includes
biographies of major figures in the field of chemistry, and provides information on
each element.
Includes bibliographical references and index.
ISBN-13: 978-0-7613-2794-3 (lib. bdg.)
ISBN-10: 0-7613-2794-0 (lib. bdg.)
1. Chemical elements—Juvenile literature.   [1. Chemical elements.]   I. Title.
QD466.M46 2006   546—dc22   2006020874

Manufactured in the United States of America
1 2 3 4 5 6 – JR – 11 10 09 08 07 06

$\mathcal{C}$ontents

Part One

The Biography of a Science

Atoma

The ancient Greeks were the first to wonder what their world was made of. Around 465 B.C. a philosopher named Democritus considered a hypothetical question. A beach, he contemplated, appears to be a solid surface, but if you look closely, you can see it is made of many millions of small grains. If you were to take one of these grains and crush it, you would get even smaller grains. Now, if you take one of these and crush it even further, you can turn it into dust. Looking very closely at this dust, you can see that it is itself made of very, very fine particles. If you rub these still more, you can reduce the dust to a fine powder. The particles of this powder are too small for your eyes to see, but is this to say that they are so small that they could not be broken into even smaller particles?

If you could keep reducing the particles to smaller and smaller pieces, there must be a point where you can go no further. You will have reduced the sand to its smallest possible particle. Democritus called these tiny, indivisible particles *atoma*, which means "something that cannot be divided."

Democritus not only gave us the idea of the **atom**—the smallest possible particle of matter—he also gave us its name. Still, he did not know exactly *what* these atoms might be, though he believed they were perfectly hard and indestructible. He thought that perhaps there might be a great many different kinds, of many different shapes. Some were smooth like marbles, some were cubical, others might have rough surfaces, and so on. Combinations of these different basic atoms, he thought, created all of the familiar materials of the world.

A bunch of rough atoms would stick together in a solid mass and become almost impossible to tear apart. This would explain why metal is hard and so difficult to cut. A mass of smooth atoms would slide around one another like a bucket full of ball bearings. Water must be made of such atoms, he decided. Other atoms would not only be smooth but so light they can float about freely. A large mass of these would account for the lightness of air. If they were also hot, they would be the flames of a fire.

Atoms, Democritus believed, are constantly combining and recombining, constantly rearranging themselves into new substances. Combinations of these atoms accounted for everything in the physical world, including his body. The air he breathed and the food he ate were made of atoms that eventually became part of his body, which was itself made of atoms. In this way, Democritus said, human beings are truly part of the ever-changing world around them.

No one, least of all Democritus, ever did any experiments to see if these ideas might actually be *true*. The ancient Greek philosophers rarely performed tests or experiments. They were more interested in ideas. Experiments were too much like work, and work was beneath the dignity of a thinker.

Unfortunately, Democritus's brilliant idea was forgotten. This was mainly because of the popularity of the ideas of a philosopher named Aristotle. Born in 384 B.C.—when Democritus was still alive—Aristotle did not believe in the notion of tiny, invisible particles called atoms.

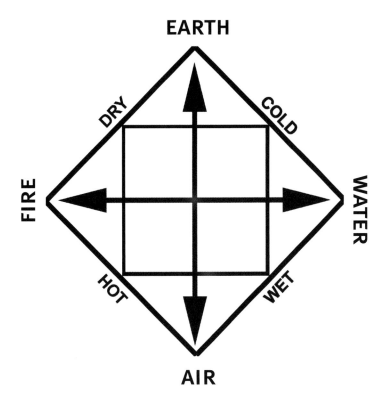

Aristotle's elements

If air and fire, he argued, were made of small, solid particles, how could they rise? They would fall to Earth like a shower of pebbles!

Instead of atoms, Aristotle proposed a simpler notion. The world was made up of just four qualities: hot, cold, wet, and dry. Combinations of these accounted for everything we see. For instance, dirt was a combination of cold and dry, water a combination of wet and cold, fire of hot and dry, and so on. If water was wet it was not because it was made of Democritus's smooth, slippery atoms, it was because it contained the quality of "wetness."

Aristotle, who wrote about almost every imaginable subject, became the standard for human science for nearly two thousand years. His word was accepted without question, even when it didn't always make much sense.

Aristotle Challenged

It was not until the seventeenth century that anyone seriously challenged Aristotle's views about the nature of the universe. This challenger was a young teacher of philosophy named Pierre Gassendi.

Gassendi thought that Aristotle's four "qualities" didn't make any sense. Aristotle said that water is made up of the qualities of cold and wet. But what, Gassendi asked, happens when water freezes? Is it now composed of new qualities, cold and dry, like rock? What if water boils and turns to steam? Is it now composed of hot and dry, like fire? And if ice and rock are composed of the same two qualities, why are they so different? One cannot melt a rock and get water or freeze water and get a rock. Gassendi had what he thought was a much better idea.

He revived Democritus's old suggestion but with some new improvements. Like many scientists of his time, Gassendi based his conclusions on a process of reasoning called induction. This involves a patient accumulation of facts, sometimes over many years, gathered by observation or experiment. Gassendi then formulated a theory.

From his observations, Gassendi concluded that instead of atoms having hundreds of different shapes, they were all pretty much alike. What made them different was how they stuck together. At first, he thought that atoms might look like tiny balls covered with little hooks. (These would cause the atoms to interlock and stick together like Velcro.) The more tightly the atoms stuck together, the tougher and harder a material was. Eventually, Gassendi came to the conclusion that instead of tiny hooks, there was a force of some kind, like magnetism, that caused atoms to stick together. This is very close to what modern scientists believe to be true.

The great scientist Isaac Newton (1642–1727) became a firm believer in the existence of atoms after reading Gassendi's books. He believed that everything was made of atoms, even light. "It seems probable to me," he wrote, "that God in the Beginning form'd Matter in solid, massy, hard, impenetrable, moveable Particles, of such Sizes and Figures, and with such other Properties, and in such Proportion to space, as most conduced to the End for which He form'd them; and that these primitive Particles being Solids, are incomparably harder than any porous Bodies compounded of them; even so very hard as never to wear or break in pieces, no ordinary Power being able to divide what God Himself made one in the First Creation."

Pierre Gassendi

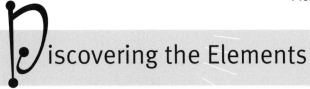iscovering the Elements

Robert Boyle, a wealthy amateur scientist in England, finally eliminated Aristotle's idea of four "elements" once and for all. He published a book in 1661 called *The Sceptical Chymist*, in which he criticized all the previous philosophers—especially Aristotle and the alchemists, who believed that gold could be made from ordinary metals like iron or lead.

Boyle said that gold could not be made—it was an "element." By this he meant that it was a basic substance that could not be composed or created from other substances. He thought that silver, copper, and mercury also were elements. In fact, Boyle was one of the first to use the word *element* in its modern sense: "I mean by elements," he wrote in 1661, "certain Primitive and Simple or perfectly intermingled bodies; which not being made of any other bodies, or of one another, are the Ingredients of which all those call'd perfectly

ALCHEMY

Often called the "father of chemistry," **alchemy** was a **pseudo-science**, that is, a false science, such as astrology. It began about the year A.D. 100 and lasted well into medieval times. Although alchemists developed many of the techniques used by chemists, their goal was the discovery of a method for turning lead and other "base" metals into gold. In spite of some genuinely valuable discoveries, they clung to the belief that all substances were combinations of sulfur, mercury, and ordinary salt, which were in turn composed of the four basic "elements" earth, air, fire, and water. Although Aristotle was not an alchemist, his work provided much of the basis for their beliefs.

mixt Bodies are immediately compounded, and into which are ultimately resolved."

Boyle wrote that all the different types of matter we see around us are composed of combinations of a small number of simple, basic substances—just as many different types of buildings, from houses to skyscrapers, can be built from a small number of basic materials. He thought that substances such as water, glass, or salt are made up of some combination of two or more elements. Moreover, he believed that it would be possible to discover the individual elements of which any substance was composed.

It was more than a century, however, before a scientist was able to do this. A French chemist named Antoine Laurent Lavoisier made this great discovery with no more complicated an instrument than a set of scales.

Lavoisier wondered what happened when something burned. Most scientists thought that objects lost weight when they burned. This seemed to make sense. After all, if you burn a piece of wood, all you are left with is a pile of fluffy ash that obviously weighs much less than the original wood. It was also a generally held belief that most materials contained a mysterious substance called phlogiston. It was thought that the release of phlogiston caused heat and light when an object burned. This, of course, was another reason to assume objects became lighter when burned.

But Lavoisier, like a good scientist, didn't take such things for granted. To determine what really happened when something burned, he burned a piece of sulfur in a sealed container. This allowed him to collect all the gases—the smoke and other vapors—released when the sulfur burned. He carefully weighed the sulfur before he burned it and then carefully weighed what was left afterward—the ash, smoke, fumes, and all. Amazingly enough, the products of the combustion weighed more than the original piece of sulfur!

Lavoisier realized what must have happened: Something combined with the sulfur when it burned. This was the gas oxygen. The combination of sulfur and oxygen weighed more than the sulfur by itself. In other words, the weight of a compound substance is the sum of the weights of the elements of which it is composed.

ANTOINE LAURENT LAVOISIER

Antoine Lavoisier

Born in Paris in 1743, Lavoisier was one of the founders of modern chemistry. In 1769 he was appointed Farmer-General of the Revenue (a kind of tax collector) and in 1776 director of the government's gunpowder mills. When the French Revolution began, people rose up against the government they felt had been oppressing them. Unfortunately for Lavoisier, tax collectors were high on the list of hated officials. The Revolutionary Tribunal sentenced him to death by guillotine. During his trial, Lavoisier pointed out the many important discoveries he had made as a scientist, but the court only said that "the Republic doesn't need scientists!" Lavoisier was executed twenty-four hours later. Later, the great French mathematician Joseph Louis Lagrange said, "It took only an instant to cut off that head, and a hundred years may not produce another like it."

Realizing that the idea of chemical elements is vital to understanding the nature of matter itself, Lavoisier compiled the first list of elements. He named twenty-eight, though only twenty-three turned out to be true elements. The remaining five included compounds and such things as "light and caloric [heat]." He also attempted to place the elements into categories according to their different properties, such as gases, metals, nonmetals, and earths. His findings were generally accepted and led to more complete lists.

Nineteenth-century chemists discovered more and more elements, especially after the discovery of electricity. It was found that when an electric current was passed through certain compounds, they would break down into their individual elements. For instance, when electricity is passed through water, it breaks down into hydrogen and oxygen. This gave scientists a new tool—**electrolysis**—for separating compounds into their individual elements. Using electrolysis, scientist Humphry Davy added sodium and potassium to the list. By the end of the century, the number of known elements had grown to eighty-two.

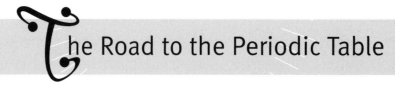

The Road to the Periodic Table

Lavoisier had divided the few elements known in the late 1700s into four classes. In the first decade of the nineteenth century, British scientist John Dalton suggested that the weight—or mass—of an atom might be its most important property. As early as 1829, German chemist Johann Dobereiner noted that similar elements often have similar **atomic weights**. In 1858 the Italian Stanislao Cannizaro determined the atomic weights for the sixty or so elements that were then known. With this sort of precise information, an early table was created in the 1860s by British chemist John Newlands. The elements were given a serial number in order of their atomic weights, beginning with hydrogen. This table made it evident that "the eighth ele-

The Biography of a Science

WHAT IS AN ELEMENT?

Everything around you—this book, the ink it is printed with, your hands, your clothes, the food you had for breakfast, and the air you are breathing—is made of one or more of the ninety-two naturally occurring elements. Everything can be broken down into simpler substances. The steel in a paper clip is a combination of iron and carbon, the water in a glass is a combination of hydrogen and oxygen, and the glass itself is mostly silicon and oxygen. But the elements *themselves* cannot be broken down into simpler substances that still retain the element's original characteristics. That is, the oxygen atom is the smallest thing that is still oxygen.

ment, starting from a given one, is a kind of repetition of the first," which Newlands called the Law of Octaves.

It was the Russian scientist Dmitri Ivanovich Mendeleyev who realized that ". . . if all the elements be arranged in order of their atomic weights a periodic repetition of properties is obtained." By this, he meant that if they were arranged properly, by atomic weight, elements with similar properties and characteristics would fall together. Elements that lie next to one another in the table would share certain qualities. He accomplished this by first writing all of the elements and their atomic weights on a series of index cards. He then began arranging the cards in different patterns. He eventually hit upon an arrangement that he liked, in which elements with similar properties were grouped in vertical columns. He published his **periodic table** and law in 1869.

One of the striking things about Mendeleyev's table is that it showed gaps—places where one might have expected an element, but for which there was none known. Mendeleyev realized that these gaps were not errors but represented elements that had not yet been discovered. The nature of his table even allowed scientists to guess at what the properties of these missing elements might be. Scientists were impressed when the elements predicted by the

Dmitri Ivanovich
Mendeleyev

table were eventually discovered and had just the properties Mendeleyev's table had predicted.

Mendeleyev's table proved to be extraordinarily accurate. In most places where Mendeleyev had difficulty in placing an element, it turned out that what was known about the element was wrong. When more accurate information became available, the problem elements fit perfectly.

The periodic table has been revised greatly over the years as scientists have learned more about the nature of the elements. Although the table usually seen in books and classrooms closely resembles Mendeleyev's original, more than seven hundred variations have been proposed, usually for special purposes (such as one designed specifically for physicists) or in special shapes that highlight certain relationships. Whatever its form, the periodic table has remained a powerful and crucial tool in science.

The Biography of a Science

Series	I	II	III	IV	V	VI	VII	VIII
1	H							
2	Li	Be	B	C	N	O	F	
3	Na	Mg	Al	Si	P	S	Cl	
4	K	Ca	Sc	Ti	V	Cr	Mn	Fe Co Ni
5	Cu	Zn	Ga	Ge	As	Se	Br	
6	Rb	Sr	Y	Zr	Nb	Mo		Ru Rh Pd
7	Ag	Cd	In	Sn	Sb	Te	I	
8	Cs	Ba	La	Ce				
9								
10			Yb		Ta	W		Os Ir Pt
11	Au	Hg	Tl	Pb	Bi			
12		Rd		Th		U		

Mendeleyev's original periodic table

THE PERIODIC TABLE

The chemical properties of an element are determined by the loosely held electrons that orbit its nucleus. Hydrogen has certain properties because it has a single electron. What differentiates one element from another is the number of protons in the nucleus. Add one proton to the nucleus of hydrogen and the atom takes on the properties of helium. Add one more proton and the atom becomes lithium. Mendeleyev noticed that certain properties reappeared in a regular order. Elements 1 through 9 are all different from one another, but number 10 is similar to number 2, number 11 to number 3, and so on. This repetition of qualities appears first at intervals of eight, and later in the system at intervals of eighteen.

The periodic table arranges the elements into seven rows or periods. The first element in any row or period is highly reactive, that is, it readily combines with other elements, while the last element in a period is almost totally nonreactive, that is, it does not easily combine with other elements. For example, potassium (K), the first element in row 4, is a very reactive substance that combines so readily with other elements that it can spontaneously burst into flame. On the other end of that row, however, is krypton (Kr), which is almost completely **inert**, rarely combining with any other element (only with extreme difficulty have chemists been able to create compounds from the heavier noble gases). Elements that lie in the vertical columns, or groups, have similar properties. For instance, the five elements in group 17—fluorine (F), chlorine (Cl), bromine (Br), iodine (I), and astatine (At)—are all part of a family known as the halogens, which means "salt forming." They are all poisonous, corrosive, and highly reactive.

Squeezed into spaces between groups two and three are the **transition elements**, which are metallic elements that chemically resemble one another extremely closely. One of these groups is called the **Lanthanide Series**, or Rare Earth Series, and the other is called the **Actinide Series**. (See the periodic table of the elements in the color insert on page 50-51.)

$\mathcal{S}$trange New Elements

In 1896 a French scientist named Henri Becquerel began investigating a nearly worthless metal called uranium—its main use was in creating a beautiful yellow glaze for ceramics. He had been researching **X-rays**, a newly discovered phenomenon that had been exciting scientists all over the world. Substances that contained uranium salts would glow after using X-rays on them. Sunlight also made uranium salts glow. In the course of his experiments, Becquerel exposed uranium salts to sunlight and then placed the salts on top of photographic plates wrapped in opaque black paper. When he developed the plates, there was a fogged area where the salts had rested.

One rainy day when there was no sunlight, he placed a sample of unexposed uranium salts on a photographic plate that had been wrapped in heavy paper, just to see what would happen. When he developed the plate, he was astonished to see a fogged area beneath where the sample had rested. It was clear to Becquerel that the uranium didn't need sunlight to activate it. It had emitted some sort of radiation entirely on its own, which had penetrated the

An old X-ray tube

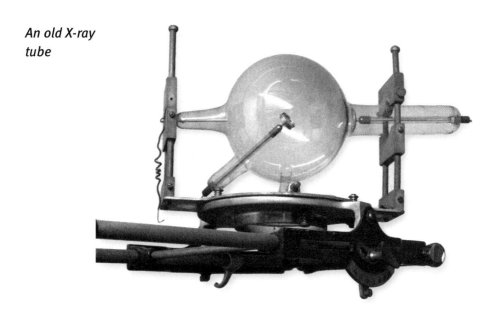

paper and exposed the plate. Becquerel had discovered what was later to become known as **radioactivity**, which is the name used to describe the emission of particles by a substance. The substances that do this are said to be radioactive.

The same year as Becquerel's discovery, a husband-and-wife team of scientists, Pierre and Marie Curie, decided to look into the cause of this mysterious radioactivity. Working with pitchblende (uranium ore), they realized that there must be some other radioactive substance in the ore besides uranium metal to account for the radioactivity they were measuring.

Marie Curie started with three tons of uranium ore. As she gradually reduced the ore into its component elements—a laborious process that took from 1899 to 1903 (she lifted every pound of ore herself)—the sample grew smaller and smaller. As it did, the radioactivity grew stronger. Finally, she separated out an entirely new element. She called it polonium after her native Poland. But even allowing for the radiation of the uranium metal itself as well as the polonium, there was still an unaccounted-for source of radioactivity remaining.

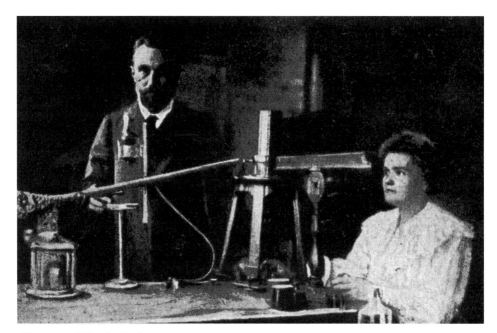

Pierre and Marie Curie

The Biography of a Science

THE CURIES

Marie Curie

Marie Curie was born Marie Sklodowska in Warsaw, Poland, in 1867. After her marriage to Pierre Curie (1859–1906), a Parisian-born chemist and physicist, she conducted research on uranium ore in his laboratory in Paris. Pierre eventually joined her in this work. Together, they discovered polonium and radium in 1898, but the amount of radium was microscopic. Later, in 1903, they managed to extract a small amount of radium from eight tons of uranium ore.

The Curies shared the 1903 Nobel Prize in Physics with Becquerel. Madame Curie continued her research after Pierre's death in a traffic accident. In 1906 she was appointed his successor to the special chair of physics at the University of Paris. She won the Nobel Prize for Chemistry in 1911, the first scientist ever to win two of these awards.

Marie Curie died in 1934 of leukemia, which is suspected to have been caused by her close work with radioactive materials.

Eventually, she reduced her original mountain of ore to a tiny sample weighing less than 0.01 ounce (0.28 gram). As small as this was, it was more than 2 million times more radioactive than an equal amount of uranium! In fact, it radiated so strongly that it glowed in the dark and was always a few degrees warmer than the surrounding air. Curie called this amazing new element radium, from the Latin word for "ray."

The Secret of Matter

Sir Ernest Rutherford

Frederick Soddy

The unusual new elements discovered by the Curies shook the foundations of physics. What was going on deep within the atoms that caused them to emit heat and strange rays that could fog photographic film and even burn human skin? Just what was this mysterious thing called radioactivity?

Research with radium eventually showed that it was emitting at least three different types of rays, which were called **alpha**, **gamma**, and **beta rays**. The beta rays were familiar: They were just streams of ordinary electrons. But what were the others? It was not until 1903 that British physicists Sir Ernest Rutherford and Frederick Soddy solved the mystery. The mysterious alpha ray, they found, was a piece, or particle, of a disintegrating atom. The atom was no longer the indestructible object imagined by Democritus.

Rutherford and Soddy's discovery completely destroyed the idea of the atom as a solid, indestructible little ball. Instead, they found that atoms are themselves made of even smaller particles. At their core is a **nucleus**. This is composed of at least one **neutron** and a **proton** (except in the case of the hydrogen atom, the

ISOTOPES

If you change the number of protons an atom has, you get an atom of an entirely different element. And when you change the number of protons, the atom will instantly find the right number of electrons to match the number of new protons. But you can change the number of neutrons in atoms all you like. Since they have no electrical charge, they do not change the chemical characteristics of the atom. Neutrons do have mass, however, so they add to the weight of an atom. An atom of hydrogen, for instance, with extra neutrons will weigh more than a normal hydrogen atom. Since an **isotope** has either fewer neutrons or more neutrons than the normal version of the atom has, the isotope of an element is usually unstable. Those with too many neutrons, for example, try to get rid of them and are therefore radioactive. Most elements come in a variety of isotopes.

nucleus of which is composed only of a single proton). **Electrons** orbit the nucleus in much the same way that the planets orbit the Sun. Electrons have a negative electrical charge and virtually no weight at all. Protons have a positive charge, and neutrons have no charge at all. The number of protons and electrons in a neutral atom is always equal. Since the electrical charge is balanced, an atom is neither positively nor negatively charged. Protons and neutrons are the heaviest parts of an atom. Their combined weights are the atomic weight of the atom.

A radium atom is 226 times heavier than a hydrogen atom. This is because the nucleus of a radium atom contains a total of 226 protons and neutrons, while that of hydrogen has only a lone proton. Therefore it's said that the atomic weight of radium is 226 and that of hydrogen is 1. An **alpha particle** weighs four times more than a hydrogen atom. So, when an atom of radium emits an alpha particle, it loses four units of weight, leaving it with an atomic weight of 222. Atoms with an atomic weight of 222 are of an entirely different chemical element, in this case, the gas radon. In giving off an alpha particle, Rutherford realized, the radium atom changed, or transmuted, into a new element. **Transmutation** is a natural process that takes place in all naturally occurring radioactive elements, such as uranium and thorium (it also occurs in radioactive artificial elements). As long as these elements continue to radiate, they will continue to gradually change into other elements.

Radium eventually transmutes into radon, but radon is also a radioactive element. Its atoms, too, are constantly emitting alpha particles. As this happens, it transforms into yet another element. Finally, after a series of successive transmutations, the original radium atom becomes an atom of lead. Lead atoms are stable; they don't emit alpha particles. A lead atom stays lead forever.

What happens to the alpha particles after they are emitted by the radium? They each have a weight of 4 atomic units. There is an element that has exactly the same weight: helium. Rutherford and Soddy wondered if alpha particles might in fact be parts of helium atoms. Examining a container of radioactive radon gas, they found that it also contained helium. The radon was not only turning into a new element, it was creating the element helium at the same time. (Most of the helium found on Earth is believed to be the result of the disintegration of naturally occurring radioactive elements in Earth's crust.) The mysterious alpha particle turned out to be the nucleus of a helium atom—two neutrons and two protons—and it was this discovery that proved that atoms were themselves made of smaller parts.

Rutherford and Soddy realized that when a radioactive atom breaks down into a new element, or **decays**, that new element may also be radioactive or it may be inert, like helium or lead. The rate at which this breakdown occurs is called the **half-life** of the element. The half-life of radium is 1,580 years, which means that in any one sample of radium, one half of the atoms will have decayed in 1,580 years. After another 1,580 years, half of the remaining sample (or one fourth of the original) will have decayed. And so on. The more radioactive an element is—that is, the more alpha and **beta**

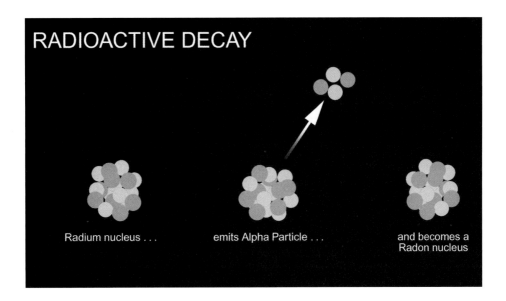

RADIOACTIVE DECAY

Radium nucleus . . .   emits Alpha Particle . . .   and becomes a
                                                                  Radon nucleus

particles it emits—the shorter its half-life is. The increased radiation is an indication of how rapidly it is transmuting into a new element. Uranium, which is much less radioactive than radium, has a half-life of more than 4 billion years, while plutonium-238 has a half-life of 87 years, and the half-life of seaborgium, which is extremely radioactive, is only 0.9 second.

Creating New Elements

In the twentieth century, scientists learned how to create new elements artificially. The first of these was technetium, which was created in 1937. A machine called a **cyclotron** was used to accelerate neutrons or alpha particles to tremendous speeds, like swinging a stone at the end of a string. These were then slammed into a sample of molybdenum. The result was an entirely new element. Interestingly, technetium fit into an open slot in the periodic table, where Mendeleyev had predicted its existence nearly seventy years earlier. It is not a stable element, however. Technetium is radioactive, so it eventually decays into a lighter element.

CYCLOTRONS AND ATOM SMASHERS

By accelerating atomic particles to tremendous speeds, scientists can slam them into atoms like tiny bullets—and just like a lightbulb hit by a bullet, the atom will shatter into many pieces. By studying the pieces, researchers can learn many things about the internal structure of atoms.

Scientists use many different machines to smash atoms, but they all work more or less the same way. A particle is accelerated by means of a series of powerful magnets, most often inside a kind of hollow donut-shaped tube. Every time the particle passes a magnet, it gets another boost. Soon it is flying through the tube at very nearly the speed of light. As soon as the particle is going as fast as they want it to, the scientists allow it to shoot off at an angle (in exactly the same way that a stone is thrown from a sling) toward its target.

Machines such as these are called accelerators because they accelerate particles to high speeds. Ones that shoot the particles around in circular paths are often called cyclotrons. Others accelerate particles down very long tunnels, like the barrel of a gun. These are called linear accelerators.

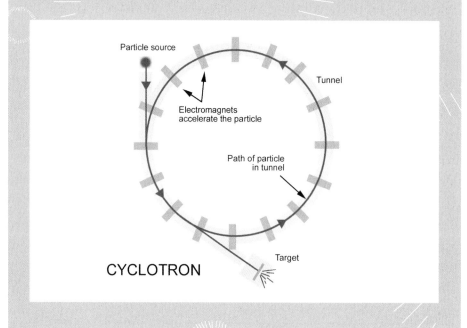

Particle source

Tunnel

Electromagnets
accelerate the particle

Path of particle
in tunnel

Target

CYCLOTRON

The Biography of a Science

Most new elements have been created this way. All of the transuranium elements, for instance, were made in laboratories. All are radioactive, some of them extremely so, and the half-lives of many are very short—in some cases, only thousandths of a second. This means that no one has ever actually seen one of these artificial elements—they simply don't last long enough.

Another method of creating artificial elements is by fusing, or combining, the nuclei of two lighter elements. For instance, elements 101 through 106 (mendelevium to seaborgium) were created by fusing the nuclei of elements such as californium with those of carbon. New elements produced in this way are created one atom at a time. This, combined with very short half-lives, from minutes to milliseconds, makes it very difficult to study the results. Sometimes there is heated debate over whether a new element was even created at all.

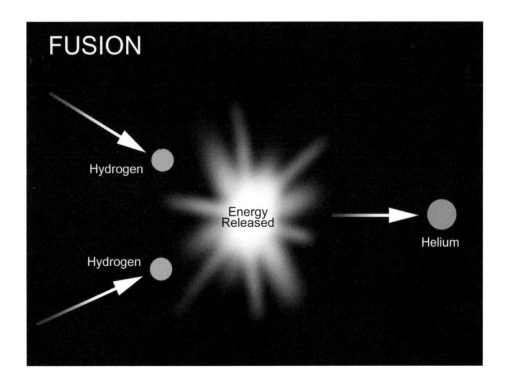

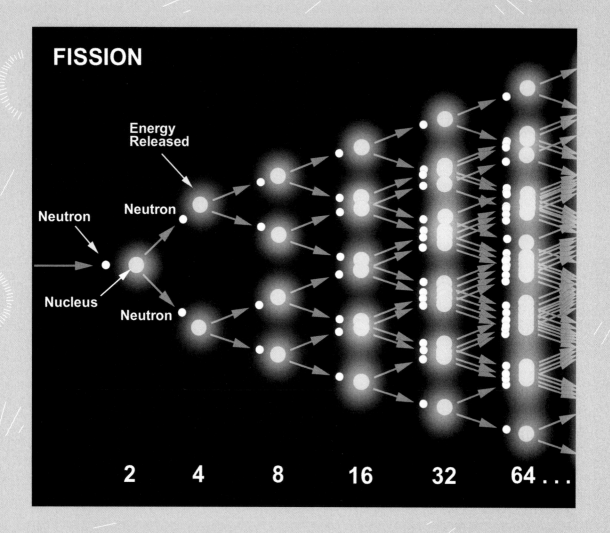

FISSION

Energy Released

Neutron

Neutron

Neutron

Nucleus

2   4   8   16   32   64 . . .

THE ATOMIC BOMB

The nucleus of an atom can fission, or split, into several smaller fragments. At the same time, two or three neutrons are emitted. The sum
of the masses of these fragments is less than the original mass. This
"missing" mass (about 0.1 percent of the original) is converted into
energy. This means that if 220 pounds (100 kilograms) of mass fissions
completely, 3.5 ounces (100 grams) will be converted into pure energy.

Fission can occur when the nucleus of a heavy atom captures a neutron, or it can happen spontaneously. If the neutrons emitted by a fissioning atom cause other atoms to fission, a chain reaction can result. For instance, if the nucleus of a splitting atom produces two neutrons, these may cause two more atoms to split, releasing four more neutrons. One atom causes two more atoms to fission, these two cause four to split, which causes eight to fission . . . and so on. This happens very rapidly, so that all of the nuclei in even a large amount of mass will almost instantly fission. This causes the release of a tremendous amount of energy.

Fission occurs naturally in the atoms of many radioactive elements. The first attempt to artificially split the nucleus of an atom occurred in 1942, when the Italian-American scientist Enrico Fermi created the first atomic reactor in a squash court at the University of Chicago. It was built of blocks of wood and uranium. Graphite—a form of carbon—was used to control the reaction. Because it absorbs neutrons, it keeps too many of them from getting loose and fissioning more uranium than might be safe.

Fermi created a controlled nuclear reaction. It did not take long for scientists to realize that an uncontrolled reaction would create a weapon of awesome power. With nothing to slow down the release of neutrons, virtually all of the energy in a mass of uranium would be released in a single microsecond, resulting in a vast explosion. The first atomic bomb was tested in the New Mexico desert in 1945.

The Road to the Atom

Democritus of Abdera (c. 460–371 B.C.) developed the idea that there is a limit to how small a sample of any substance could get. He called this tiny, solid, indivisible particle atoma, which means "something that cannot be divided." He also believed that there are four different kinds of atoms—one each for earth, air, fire, and water—and that all substances are simply combinations of these. Atoms, Democritus stated, come in all weights, shapes, and colors. "Some are rough," he wrote, "some hook-shaped, some concave, some convex, and some have other innumerable variations." The atoms of water, for instance, must be very slippery and smooth, while those of earth must be rough and sticky so rocks and metals will hold together.

Pierre Gassendi (1592–1655) revived the atom idea, which had lain dormant for many centuries. Where Democritus held that different substances were created by various mixtures of the four basic elements, Gassendi introduced the concept of the **molecule**, or individual group of atoms. He believed they were held together by tiny hooks.

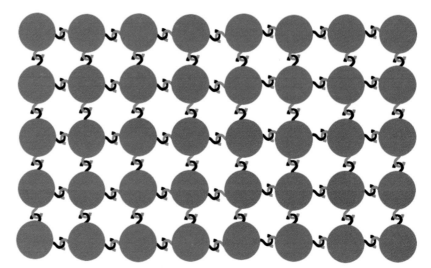

When Antonie van Leeuwenhoek (1632–1723) began using the newly invented microscope in 1670, an entire world was revealed that had never been suspected. His discoveries showed that there were indeed things that were smaller than the human eye could see. If there were creatures so small that hundreds could fit on the head of a pin, was the idea of the even smaller atom so impossible?

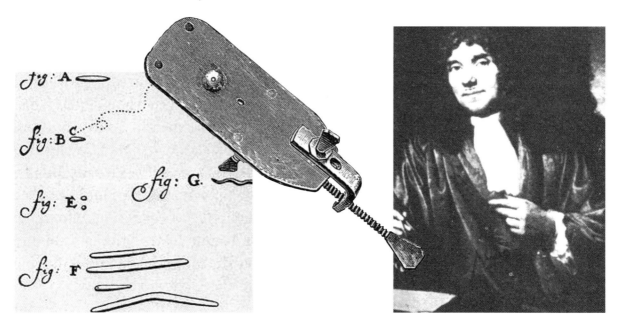

The Road to the Atom

Robert Boyle (1627–1691) introduced the concept of the chemical element. These were real, physical substances such as gold that could not be separated into simpler substances.

John Dalton (1766–1844) reintroduced the idea of the atom in 1803, though a few scientists and philosophers before him had kept Democritus's ideas alive. He abandoned the idea of little hooks and other attachments and assumed that some type of force held atoms together, as

though they were tiny magnets. He thought that the way in which atoms grouped together determined the qualities of different types of matter. Copper atoms, he suggested, bonded into regular squares. When millions of these squares stuck together, they formed solid crystals. And when millions of these crystals combined, they formed the copper metal everyone is familiar with. Just as there are special atoms of copper, Dalton said, there is a particular atom for every one of the chemical elements. Every atom of an element is exactly alike and is unlike the atoms of any other element.

The great British physicist Isaac Newton (1642–1727) supported the idea of atoms, even suggesting that light itself is composed of individual particles.

Dalton's ideas about the atom are not much different from those of Boyle or Gassendi, or even Democritus, for that matter, but one of his most important contributions was his explanation of how atoms combined to form different substances. Atoms can combine only in certain fixed proportions, Dalton said. For example, one unit of hydrogen mixed with eight units of oxygen produces nine units of water. It was just like using two different types of tile to create a pattern on a floor. If you have the right proportions of colors you get the pattern you want.

Dalton assumed, however, that one unit of hydrogen—whether that be one ounce or one kilogram—contains the same number of atoms as eight similar units of oxygen, so that the atoms are joined one to one: one hydrogen atom to one oxygen atom: H-O.

The only problem with Dalton's theory is that it only *assumed* that the number of atoms is the same in the two different quantities of gas. If they weren't, then the formula for water could be just about anything: H_4O or HO_3 or even H_2O.

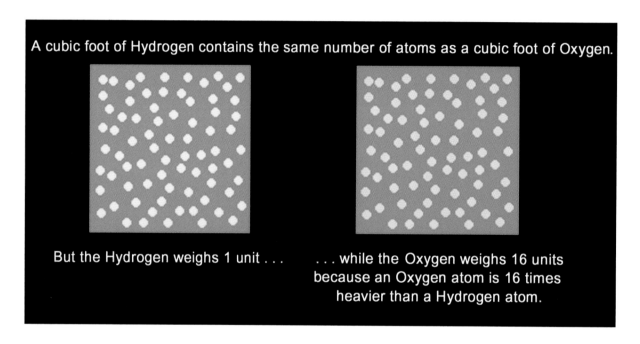

A cubic foot of Hydrogen contains the same number of atoms as a cubic foot of Oxygen.

But the Hydrogen weighs 1 unit . . .

. . . while the Oxygen weighs 16 units because an Oxygen atom is 16 times heavier than a Hydrogen atom.

The Italian physicist Amadeo Avogadro (1776–1856) solved this problem with the theory that like quantities of any two gases contain the same number of atoms. That is, one unit of hydrogen contains the same number of atoms as one unit of oxygen—or any other gas, for that matter. He knew that oxygen weighs sixteen times more than a like quantity of hydrogen. If the number of atoms is the same, then an atom of oxygen must weigh sixteen times more than an atom of hydrogen. Therefore there would be, Avogadro reasoned, the same number of atoms in a half unit of hydrogen as in eight units of oxygen. Since Dalton's recipe for water required one unit of hydrogen and eight units of oxygen, this meant that the water molecule must consist of two hydrogen atoms and one oxygen atom—and the correct formula for water must be H_2O.

The Road to the Atom

For a long time scientists believed that the atom was a solid object, like a marble or ball bearing. But while studying radioactive substances in 1909, British physicist Sir Ernest Rutherford made an astonishing discovery. He had been shooting a (alpha) particles emitted from a sample of uranium through a sheet of thin gold foil. The particles passed through the gold as though it weren't there! This would be impossible if the atoms of gold were solid objects. Then he made an even more amazing discovery: Every once in a while one of the alpha particles would shoot out of the gold foil at an odd angle, as though it had bounced off something. Rutherford reasoned that atoms must be thin, empty shells surrounding a tiny, solid nucleus. It was the stray alpha particle hitting the tiny inner nucleus that had revealed its existence.

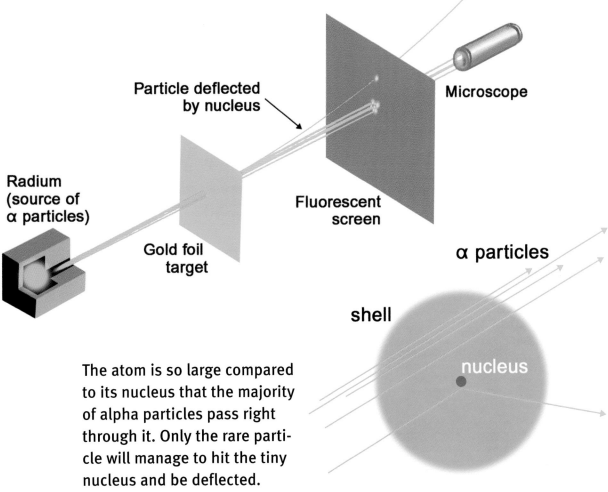

Particle deflected by nucleus

Microscope

Radium (source of α particles)

Fluorescent screen

Gold foil target

α particles

shell

nucleus

The atom is so large compared to its nucleus that the majority of alpha particles pass right through it. Only the rare particle will manage to hit the tiny nucleus and be deflected.

The Road to the Atom

In 1913, Danish physicist Niels Bohr refined the concept of the atom even further. Instead of a shell, the nucleus was surrounded by one or more electrons orbiting it like planets around the Sun. Every atom, Bohr said, was made of only two different basic particles: the electron, which has a negative electrical charge, and the proton, which has a positive charge. Hydrogen, the simplest of all atoms, has only one of each. Helium has two protons in its nucleus and two orbiting electrons; lithium, the third heaviest element, has three of each; and so on to very heavy elements such as gold, which has 79 protons and 79 electrons. For every proton in the nucleus of an atom, there are an equal number of electrons.

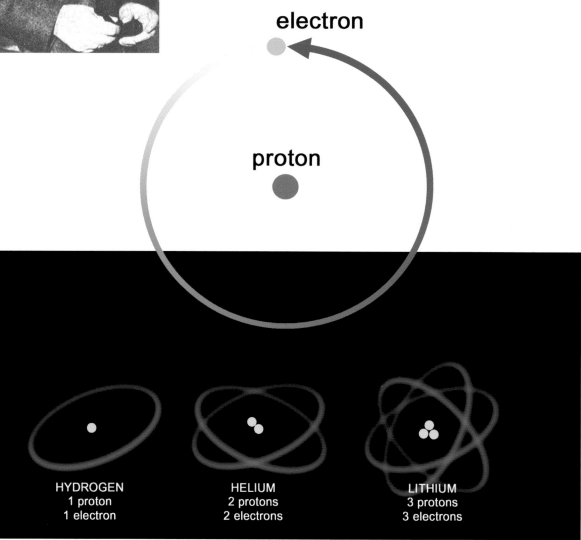

electron

proton

HYDROGEN
1 proton
1 electron

HELIUM
2 protons
2 electrons

LITHIUM
3 protons
3 electrons

ANATOMY OF AN ATOM

An entirely new particle was discovered in 1932: the neutron. This is a particle with no electrical charge at all, which goes toward explaining why it took so long before anyone found it. It does not react much—if at all—with other particles. The nucleus of every atom except hydrogen contains neutrons. The nucleus of the helium atom contains two protons and two electrons; that of lithium, three protons and four neutrons. When an atom contains more than the normal number of neutrons it is called an isotope. Oxygen can come in any one of three different isotopes, and the metal tin has ten. Extra neutrons don't change the type of element—that is determined by the number of electrons. All neutrons do is change the overall weight of the atom. They can, however, change the characteristics of an element so that it reacts differently chemically. Many isotopes are radioactive, too, as the atoms of that element try to get rid of their excess neutrons.

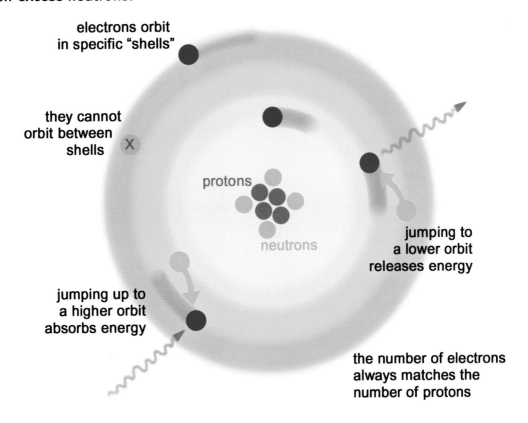

electrons orbit
in specific "shells"

they cannot
orbit between
shells

protons

neutrons

jumping to
a lower orbit
releases energy

jumping up to
a higher orbit
absorbs energy

the number of electrons
always matches the
number of protons

This diagram cannot show the parts of the atom to their true scale. In reality an atom is mostly empty space.

If the red dot is the nucleus of a typical atom, the nearest electrons would be orbiting a mile away.

EVER SMALLER . . .

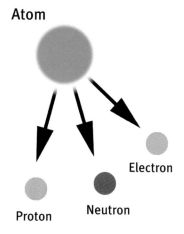

Atom

Electron

Proton

Neutron

Until the 1960s, it was thought that the atom consisted of just three smaller—or **subatomic**—particles: electrons, protons, and neutrons. Physicists studying the interior of the atom with powerful machines such as cyclotrons discovered many other subatomic particles: photons, neutrinos, muons, kaons, and so forth. The atom, however, is composed of just three of these: electrons, protons, and neutrons. Then, in 1963, physicists Murray Gell-Mann and George Zweigof proposed the existence of even smaller particles, which they called **quarks**.

Neutrons and protons are each made of three quarks. No one has observed quarks as individual particles, though they have been detected indirectly.

Particles that are made of quarks are called **hadrons**.

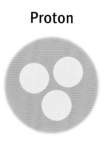

Proton

Neutron

Electrons, however, are a type of particle called a **lepton**, which is not made of quarks. Like the original concept of the atom, leptons are believed to be indivisible. Leptons are all lightweight particles. With the exception of the stable electron and neutrino, leptons are also very short-lived, with most of them existing for only a millionth of a second or less. The neutrino has so little mass and reacts with matter so weakly, that one of them can pass through the entire Earth without notice.

All matter is thought to be made up of quarks—which come in eighteen different varieties—and leptons, along with the forces that hold them together. Are quarks made of even smaller particles? Most physicists don't think so, but then, a hundred years ago, most physicists thought the same thing about the atom. . . .

The Road to the Atom

Radiation

Sir William Crookes studied a strange effect that had been discovered in the late nineteenth century.

Sir William Crookes in his laboratory

This involved a glass tube with a wire embedded in each end. A current was then sent through the wire.

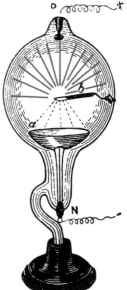

There was a flow of electrical current from the negative **cathode** to the positive **anode**. This flow was called the **cathode ray**.

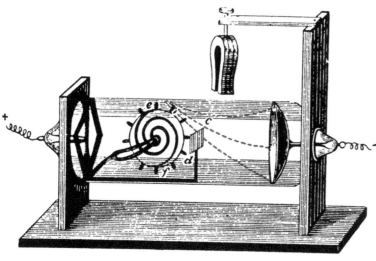

Crookes was very curious about the nature of this energy. What was it? He performed a great many experiments on what he called "radiant matter."

When the flow was blocked by the plate at *d*, the wheel would stop turning. But a magnet placed nearby would deflect the ray, causing the wheel to spin again. This experiment proved that the cathode ray had both mass, because it was able to turn the wheel, and an electrical charge, because it could be affected by the magnet.

If these were particles being emitted by the cathode, what were they and where did they come from?

In 1895 the German scientist Wilhelm Konrad Roentgen discovered a new ray being emitted by a special type of Crookes tube he had been experimenting with. He found that this mysterious ray could pass directly through human flesh, creating a shadow of the bones on a photographic plate. He called these mysterious rays X-rays. While doctors immediately put the X-ray to use in medicine, other scientists tried to discover just what these strange rays were and where they came from.

Crookes tube

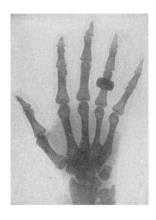

An early X-ray apparatus and an X-ray image of a person's hand taken at the turn of the twentieth century

In 1896, while searching for the source of the mysterious X-rays, French scientist Henri Becquerel discovered a strange property of uranium that he called radioactivity.

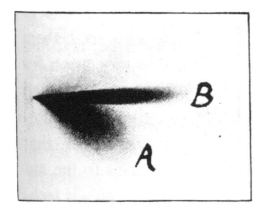

He discovered that uranium left an image on photographic film just as X-rays did. The uranium, he realized, must be emitting rays of some kind. They must be similar to the rays created by the Crookes tube, because they could be diverted by a magnetic field. What was the source of this mysterious radiation?, Becquerel wondered.

A piece of uranium fogged this film, but a strong magnet diverted the rays in two different directions.

Radiation

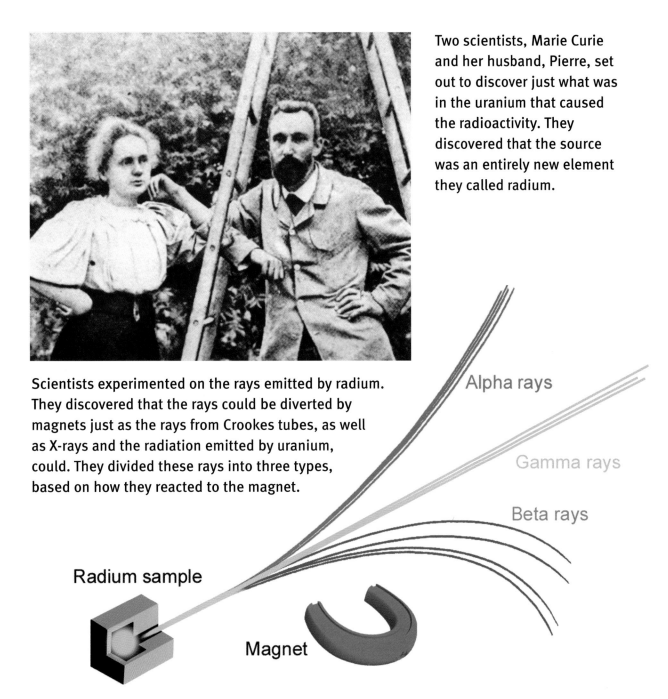

Two scientists, Marie Curie and her husband, Pierre, set out to discover just what was in the uranium that caused the radioactivity. They discovered that the source was an entirely new element they called radium.

Scientists experimented on the rays emitted by radium. They discovered that the rays could be diverted by magnets just as the rays from Crookes tubes, as well as X-rays and the radiation emitted by uranium, could. They divided these rays into three types, based on how they reacted to the magnet.

Alpha rays

Gamma rays

Beta rays

Radium sample

Magnet

The big mystery for scientists now was the nature of these rays. What were they and where did they come from? It was eventually discovered that they were pieces of disintegrating atoms. Alpha particles were the same as the nucleus of the helium atom: two protons and two neutrons. Beta rays were composed of single particles that turned out to be electrons. Gamma rays, the most powerful of the three, are a relative of the X-ray.

But what happened to the original atom as it broke down and released these particles? Scientists realized that the atom itself must be changed in some way as it loses pieces of itself.

Alpha particles are made up of two protons and two neutrons. A radium atom has an atomic weight of 226, or 226 times the weight of a hydrogen atom. An alpha particle weighs four times as much as a hydrogen atom. When a radium atom loses an alpha particle as radiation, it also loses four units of weight. Its atomic weight is now 222. Atoms with that atomic weight are an entirely different element—in this case, radon, a heavy, radioactive gas.

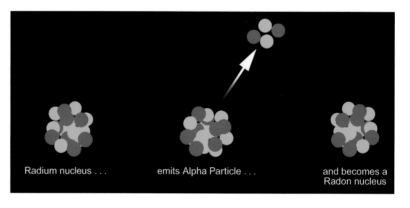

Radium nucleus . . .   emits Alpha Particle . . .   and becomes a Radon nucleus

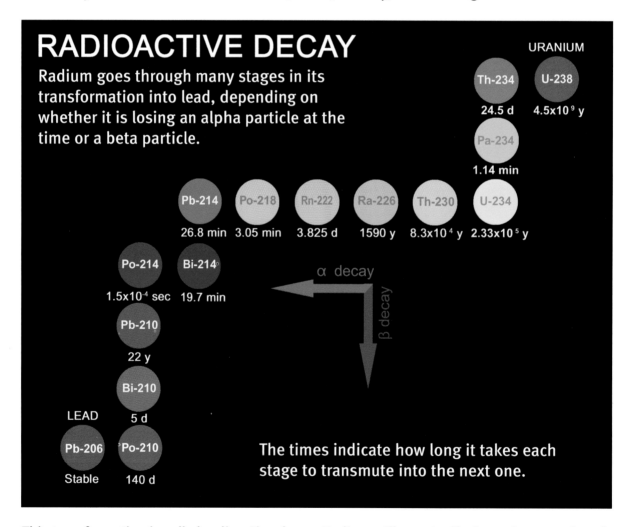

RADIOACTIVE DECAY

URANIUM

Radium goes through many stages in its transformation into lead, depending on whether it is losing an alpha particle at the time or a beta particle.

Th-234   U-238

24.5 d   4.5x10⁹ y

Pa-234

1.14 min

Pb-214   Po-218   Rn-222   Ra-226   Th-230   U-234

26.8 min 3.05 min 3.825 d   1590 y   8.3x10⁴ y 2.33x10⁵ y

Po-214   Bi-214

1.5x10⁻⁴ sec 19.7 min

α decay

β decay

Pb-210

22 y

Bi-210

LEAD   5 d

Pb-206   Po-210

Stable   140 d

The times indicate how long it takes each stage to transmute into the next one.

This transformation is called radioactive decay. Radium will eventually decay into a series of elements, each slightly lighter than the previous one, until it eventually turns into lead. Since lead is not radioactive, it is stable and the decay stops.

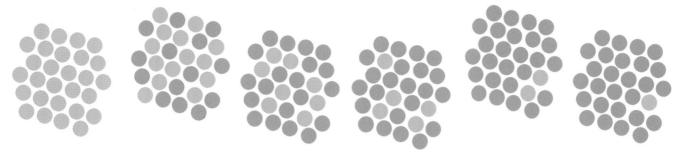

It is not possible to guess exactly *when* any individual atom will decay. However, the time required for a large number of atoms to decay can be determined. Scientists put it this way: one half of a given number of radioactive atoms will decay over a given amount of time. This period is called the half-life of that element. For example, the half-life of radium is about 1,580 years. This means that if you had a pound of radium, 1,580 years later you would have only half a pound. The rest will have decayed into lead. After another 1,580 years you would have only a quarter pound, and so on. After every 1,580 years, your sample of radium will have decayed by half.

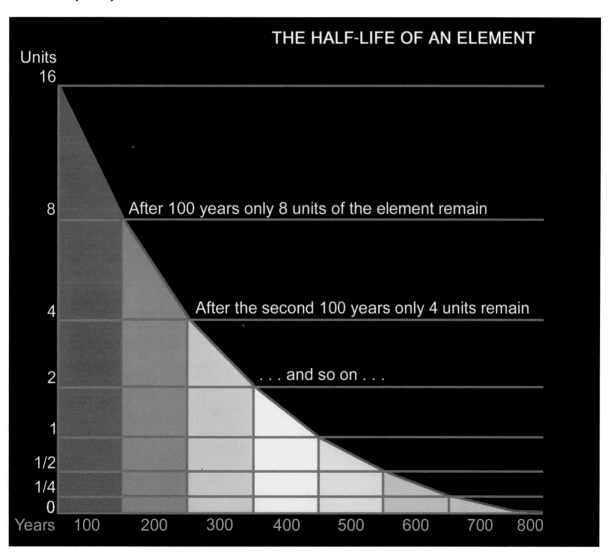

THE HALF-LIFE OF AN ELEMENT

Units

After 100 years only 8 units of the element remain

After the second 100 years only 4 units remain

. . . and so on . . .

16
8
4
2
1
1/2
1/4
0

Years   100   200   300   400   500   600   700   800

HALF-LIFE EXPERIMENT

Needed:
Large sheet of paper and a pen or pencil
100 pennies or other coins
Bowl or other small container

With the pen or pencil, divide the paper into vertical columns. Mix up the pennies in the container and dump them onto a table. Take all of the pennies that landed heads up and place them in the first column. Put all of the other pennies back into the container and toss them again. Take all of the pennies that landed heads up this time and put them in the second column. Keep repeating this until all the pennies are used up.

Even though it is impossible to tell which way any *individual* penny will fall, the chances of it landing heads up are 50 percent. So about half the pennies in each toss will end up in a column. After the first toss you will have about half the pennies you started with, then a quarter, then an eighth, and so on. This means that the half-life of the container of pennies is one toss since each toss removes about half the pennies.

Radiation

USEFUL RADIATION

Many scientists, such as archaeologists, who study ancient humans, have made good use of knowing the half-life of certain elements. A radioactive form of carbon known as carbon-14 is known to have a half-life of 5,700 years. This means that after 5,700 years, an object will have only half the amount of carbon-14 it started with. If the original amount is known, this would make it possible to determine the age of the object. For example, if an object had only one quarter the original amount, it would be 11,400 years old.

Carbon-14 is always present in Earth's atmosphere. It combines with oxygen to form carbon dioxide, just as normal, stable carbon (carbon-12) does. Plants absorb this carbon dioxide during photosynthesis. The plants are then eaten by animals and people. Because the ratio of carbon-14 to carbon-12 in the atmosphere is always about the same, the amount of these two forms of carbon in living organisms is always about the same, too. The carbon-14 that decays into carbon-12 is constantly being replaced by new carbon-14.

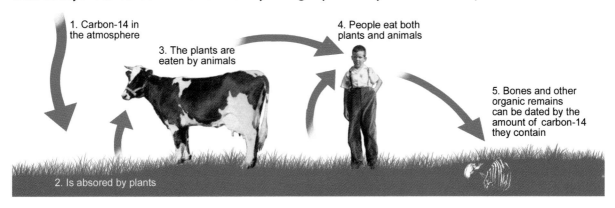

1. Carbon-14 in the atmosphere

3. The plants are eaten by animals

4. People eat both plants and animals

5. Bones and other organic remains can be dated by the amount of carbon-14 they contain

2. Is absorbed by plants

When an organism dies, it stops taking in carbon-14. The carbon-14 in the organism continues to decay but it is not replaced by new carbon-14. The ratio of the two forms of carbon begins to change. By measuring the proportion of carbon-14 to carbon-12 in a sample, such as a fossil bone, and comparing it to the ratio in a living organism, scientists can tell how long ago the sample lived.

Almost any formerly living substance can be dated this way, although carbon-14 dating is not very accurate for things older than about 60,000 years. For older samples, the proportions of radioactive elements with longer half-lives, such as potassium-40, are measured.

DANGEROUS RADIATION

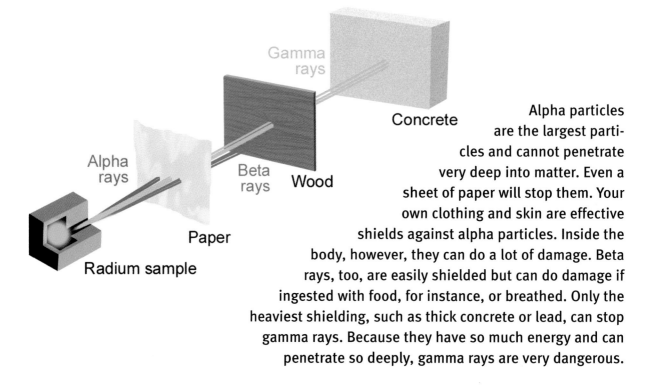

Gamma rays

Concrete

Beta rays

Wood

Alpha rays

Paper

Radium sample

Alpha particles are the largest particles and cannot penetrate very deep into matter. Even a sheet of paper will stop them. Your own clothing and skin are effective shields against alpha particles. Inside the body, however, they can do a lot of damage. Beta rays, too, are easily shielded but can do damage if ingested with food, for instance, or breathed. Only the heaviest shielding, such as thick concrete or lead, can stop gamma rays. Because they have so much energy and can penetrate so deeply, gamma rays are very dangerous.

RADON

One of the by-products of the decay of uranium is the radioactive gas radon. Since uranium occurs naturally in the Earth, especially in soils containing shale and granite, radon is constantly being produced as the uranium decays naturally. Radon gas can penetrate entire buildings through cracks in basement walls, floors, and other openings. It can also seep into wells. As radon decays, it emits high-energy alpha particles. Because these are breathed or ingested with food or water, they can be very dangerous to human health. The American Lung Association believes that radon may be second only to smoking as a cause of lung cancer. Fortunately, kits can be purchased that allow homeowners to easily test for radon in their homes. If radon is discovered, levels can be lowered by sealing cracks and increasing air flow through the contaminated area.

The Elements
In and Around Us

Light elements such as hydrogen and helium are fused into heavier elements under the tremendous heat and pressure deep within the furnace of a star's interior. If a star explodes, these heavy elements are scattered into the universe, where they eventually combine to create clouds of dust, planets, and perhaps even living creatures such as yourself.

PERIODIC TABLE OF THE ELEMENTS

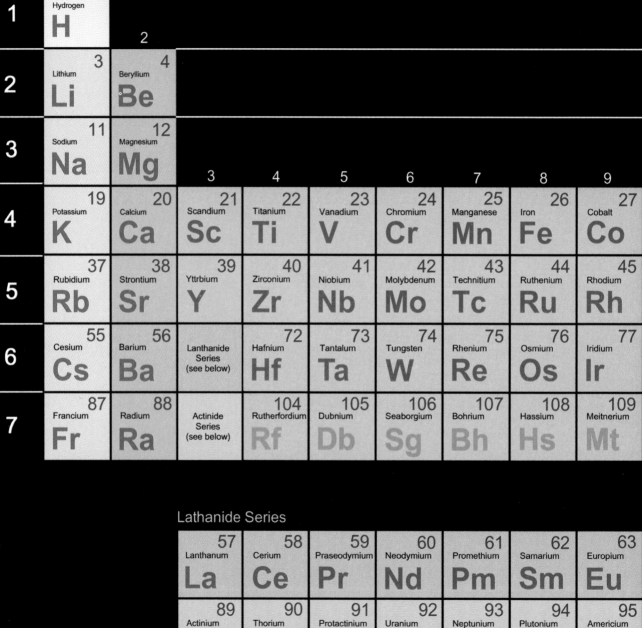

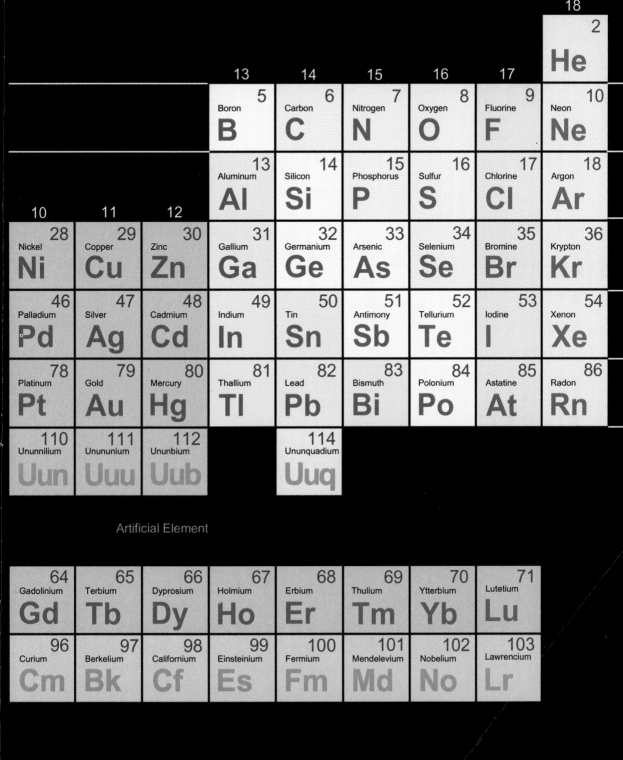

18

2
He

13 14 15 16 17

5 Boron B | 6 Carbon C | 7 Nitrogen N | 8 Oxygen O | 9 Fluorine F | 10 Neon Ne

13 Aluminum Al | 14 Silicon Si | 15 Phosphorus P | 16 Sulfur S | 17 Chlorine Cl | 18 Argon Ar

10 11 12

28 Nickel Ni | 29 Copper Cu | 30 Zinc Zn | 31 Gallium Ga | 32 Germanium Ge | 33 Arsenic As | 34 Selenium Se | 35 Bromine Br | 36 Krypton Kr

46 Palladium Pd | 47 Silver Ag | 48 Cadmium Cd | 49 Indium In | 50 Tin Sn | 51 Antimony Sb | 52 Tellurium Te | 53 Iodine I | 54 Xenon Xe

78 Platinum Pt | 79 Gold Au | 80 Mercury Hg | 81 Thallium Tl | 82 Lead Pb | 83 Bismuth Bi | 84 Polonium Po | 85 Astatine At | 86 Radon Rn

110 Ununnilium Uun | 111 Unununium Uuu | 112 Ununbium Uub | 114 Ununquadium Uuq

Artificial Element

64 Gadolinium Gd | 65 Terbium Tb | 66 Dyprosium Dy | 67 Holmium Ho | 68 Erbium Er | 69 Thulium Tm | 70 Ytterbium Yb | 71 Lutetium Lu

96 Curium Cm | 97 Berkelium Bk | 98 Californium Cf | 99 Einsteinium Es | 100 Fermium Fm | 101 Mendelevium Md | 102 Nobelium No | 103 Lawrencium Lr

Metalloids   Halogens   Noble Gases   Lanthanide Series   Actinide Series

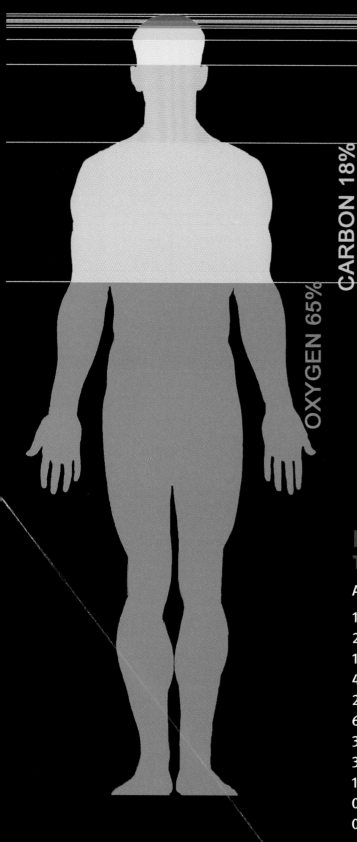

OXYGEN 65%

CARBON 18%

HYDROGEN 10%

NITROGEN 3%

CALCIUM 1.5%

PHOSPHORUS 1%

POTASSIUM 0.35%

SULFUR 0.25%

SODIUM 0.15%

MAGNESIUM 0.05%

Co, Zn, Se, Mo, F, Cl, I, Mn, Co, Fe 0.7 %
Li, Sr, Al, Si, Pb, V, As, Br Trace Amounts

ELEMENTS IN THE HUMAN BODY

A body weighing 154 pounds (70 kilograms) contains:

100.31 pounds (45.5 kilograms) of oxygen
27.78 pounds (12.6 kilograms) of carbon
15.43 pounds (7 kilograms) of hydrogen
4.62 pounds (2.1 kilograms) of nitrogen
2.31 pounds (1.05 kilogram) of calcium
6.08 ounces (0.175 kilogram) of sulfur
3.68 ounces (0.105 kilogram) of sodium
3.68 ounces (0.105 kilogram) of chlorine
1.23 ounces (0.035 kilogram) of magnesium
0.0099 ounce (0.00028 kilogram) of iron
0.00099 ounce (0.000028 kilogram) of iodine

FLUORINE
Prevents tooth decay

FRUITS
Iron, selenium

MOLYBDENUM
In enzymes

DAIRY PRODUCTS
Calcium, magnesium,
phosphorus, sulphur

CALCIUM
Bones and teeth

IODINE
Thyroid gland

SELENIUM
Thyroid gland

CHROMIUM
Blood sugar level

PHOSPHORUS
pH balance

CEREALS & BREAD
Chromium, copper, iron,
manganese, molybdenum,
zinc, potassium, sulfur

ZINC
In enzymes

COPPER
In enzymes

CHLORINE
Water balance,
stomach acid

IRON
Blood

MANGANESE
Bones

POTASSIUM
Muscle functions, nerves

SULFUR
Proteins

MEATS, FISH & NUTS
Chromium, copper, fluoride,
iron, manganese, magnesium,
selenium, phosphorus,
potassium, sulfur

COBALT
In vitamin B-12

VEGETABLES
Iron, manganese, molybdenum,
selenium, cobalt

Your body is not only made of elements,
many of them play a vital role in its
functions and health. A good diet
ensures that you get the elements
your body requires.

AROUND THE HOUSE

Many familiar household products are elements or simple compounds of only two or three elements. Ordinary table salt is one of the most familiar examples. It consists of only two elements: a violently reactive metal, sodium, and a poisonous gas, chlorine. Since iodine is an important part of nutrition, it is often added to table salt. Baking soda (sodium bicarbonate) is a combination of four elements: sodium, hydrogen, carbon, and oxygen. The silvery liquid in old thermometers is mercury—a metallic element now banned from most household uses because it is extremely poisonous. Modern thermometers use tinted alcohol instead. Other common products that are simple combinations of elements include ammonia, which consists of one atom each of nitrogen and oxygen and three atoms of hydrogen; and mothballs, whose molecules are each made of ten carbon atoms and eight hydrogen atoms.

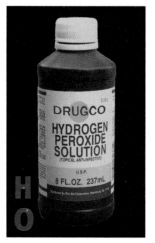

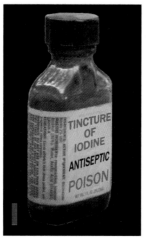

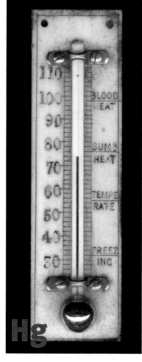

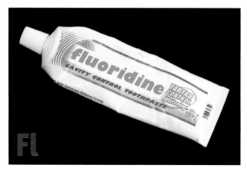

Hydrogen peroxide, an effective disinfectant, is made of two atoms of hydrogen and two of oxygen. Another disinfectant, iodine, consists of iodine crystals dissolved in alcohol. Fluorine helps make tooth enamel strong, so a compound containing fluorine is added to many toothpastes and sometimes to a city's drinking water. Milk of magnesia, which contains magnesium, is used to calm upset stomachs and relieve diarrhea.

Glass is composed primarily of silica, a combination of silicon and oxygen. Another familiar form of silica is ordinary beach sand.

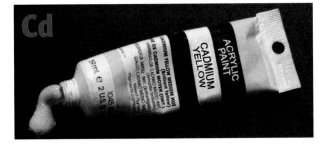

Tungsten has the highest melting point of any metal, so it is commonly used for the filament in lightbulbs. Phosphorus is used in making the heads of matches. Ordinary blackboard chalk is calcium carbonate, a combination of calcium, carbon, and oxygen atoms.

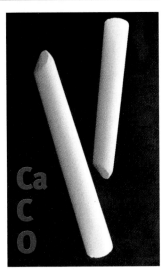

The compounds of many elements, such as cadmium and chrome, produce beautiful colors and are used in the manufacture of paints. Both titanium and lead have been used in making white paint, though lead has been banned from use in most paints because it is highly poisonous.

SCIENCE, NATURE, AND INDUSTRY

Above left to right: Elements such as silicon, germanium, and copper are important ingredients in the creation of modern electronics such as this circuit board. Copper is one of the most important metallic elements. It can be found everywhere in your home from the wiring to the plumbing. Nickel is another familiar metal, though it is rarely used in its pure state. The nickname for the five-cent coin comes from the large amount of nickel used in it.

Oxygen and hydrogen are two of the most abundant elements on Earth. Necessary for animal life, most of the free oxygen in our atmosphere is produced by **photosynthesis** in plants.

When hydrogen is burned—that is, combined with oxygen—it produces water. The three main engines of the space shuttle (the three glowing circles at the rear of the shuttle itself) burn hydrogen and oxygen, so the exhaust is nothing but ordinary steam. This is why there is no visible flame or smoke from these engines. The solid fuel boosters, on the other hand, burn a fuel rich in powdered aluminum and produce a huge flame and great amounts of smoke.

Part Two

The Lore of the Elements

#1

Hydrogen

H

Discovery: Henry Cavendish in 1766

Origin of name: Coined by Antoine Lavoisier, the word hydrogen is derived from the Greek *hydro genes*, which means "water forming," because when hydrogen burns it combines with oxygen to form water.

Hydrogen is a colorless, odorless gas. When hydrogen burns it combines with oxygen, producing water. Liquid hydrogen is used as the fuel for the main engines of the space shuttle, so what you see coming out of the main engines of the space shuttle is ordinary steam!

Hydrogen is the simplest of all the elements and the simplest possible atom. Its nucleus is composed of only a single proton, which is orbited by only a single electron. This is the reason that hydrogen is also the lightest of all the elements.

Hydrogen is the most abundant element in the universe. Stars are composed mostly of hydrogen, and it is the fusion of hydrogen atoms into helium atoms that releases the energy that makes stars shine. The planet Jupiter is composed mostly of hydrogen. Because hydrogen is so light, most of Earth's original hydrogen escaped into space because Earth's gravity was too weak to hold on to it. What didn't escape combined with other elements—oxygen for the most part. Today on our planet, hydrogen is found in the greatest quantities combined with oxygen in the form of water. Hydrogen is the main constituent of water, which is composed of two atoms of hydrogen and

▲ *Hydrogen, being generated in the tanks on the left, inflates a Civil War observation balloon.*

one of oxygen. This is reflected in its chemical formula: H_2O. Free hydrogen is found in the atmosphere only in very small amounts: less than 1 part per million by volume.

Hydrogen is used to make such key materials as methane, ammonia, cyclohexane, and methanol, which are used in the production of fertilizers, plastics, and pharmaceuticals. Because hydrogen can be separated from water and, when it burns, produces only water as a waste product, some people predict that hydrogen gas will be the clean fuel of the future.

Atomic weight: 1
Melting point: −434.5°F (−259°C)

#2

Helium

He

Discovery: Pierre Janssen in 1868

Origin of name: It comes from *helios*, the Greek word for the Sun.

Although helium occurs naturally on Earth, it was discovered in the Sun. It was first detected during the solar eclipse of 1868, when astronomer Pierre Janssen saw a previously unnoticed line in the solar **spectrum** that could not be explained by any known element. Helium was not found on this planet until 1895, when William Ramsay discovered some in a sample of uranium ore. Today, most helium is obtained from natural gas wells.

Helium is one of the six elements known as the noble gases because they are so inert. Helium will not combine with any other element—not even itself. While hydrogen and oxygen, for instance, are normally found as molecules each composed of two atoms—H_2 and O_2—helium is found only as single atoms. It is also one of the least dense gases, second only to hydrogen. For this reason, it is used in balloons and blimps. Its lifting power is not as great as hydrogen's, but helium is much safer since it is nonflammable.

Helium is the second most abundant element in the universe, after hydrogen. It is not found in Earth's atmosphere. All of the helium used on this planet is extracted commercially from natural gas wells.

Atomic weight: 4
Melting point: −457.96°F (−272.2°C)

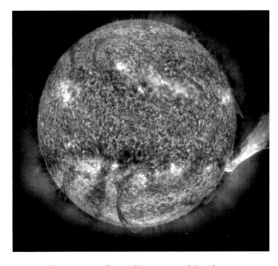

▲ *Helium was first discovered in the spectrum of the Sun. Atoms of helium, the second lightest element, are the result of the fusion of hydrogen atoms—the process by which the Sun's light and heat are created. (NASA)*

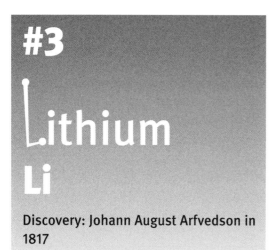

#3
Lithium
Li

Discovery: Johann August Arfvedson in 1817

Origin of name: The name comes from *lithos,* the Greek word for "rock."

Pure lithium must be kept in oil to prevent it from coming into contact with air or water.

Silvery lithium is the lightest of all the metals. It reacts strongly with oxygen, so it is usually stored in oil. It is so light that it will float on water, but when it comes into contact with water, it combines rapidly with the oxygen, releasing hydrogen in the process. Because it **oxidizes** so readily, it is almost never found in its pure form in nature. It is, however, found in most igneous (volcanic) rocks and in the water of many mineral springs, which accounts for its name.

Lithium is a member of the group called the **alkali metals**, which are all very reactive. As their **atomic number** increases, so does their reactivity. Lithium, with an atomic number of 3, is the least reactive of the group. Cesium, an alkali metal with an atomic number of 55, will actually explode in contact with water.

While lithium is almost never used in its pure form (it is so soft it can be cut with a knife), its **compounds** and alloys are very useful. A lightweight lithium-aluminum alloy is used in building aircraft and spacecraft.

Lithium is also used in spacecraft in the form of lithium hydroxide, which absorbs carbon dioxide from the air. On the other hand, lithium chromide absorbs water very well, so it is useful in air-conditioning and drying systems. Lithium is also used in greases (as lithium stearate), batteries, ceramics, and glass.

Although it has no known biological role, lithium is an important ingredient in medications used to treat depression. When taken in the form of lithium carbonate, it interferes with the chemical messengers by which nerves communicate with each other. Lithium also affects the concentrations of different hormones in the brain. In addition, lithium increases the production of white blood cells in the bone marrow.

Atomic weight: 6.941
Melting point: approximately 355.7°F (179.85°C)

The Lore of the Elements

#4

Beryllium
Be

Discovery: Louis-Nicolas Vauquelin in 1798

Origin of name: It is named for the gemstone beryl, in which it was found.

◄ *Beryllium*

▲ *Emerald in its natural crystal form and as a cut gem*

Beryllium was discovered combined with oxygen in the form of beryllium oxide. The lightweight, steel-gray metal itself was not isolated until 1828.

Beryllium, which is almost never found in the free state because it is too reactive, is a relatively scarce metal. It is nonmagnetic and has one of the lowest densities—which means that it is very lightweight—and highest melting points of all metals. It is most useful mixed with other metals as an **alloy**. Beryllium copper, for instance, is used for springs, electrical contacts, spot-welding electrodes, and nonsparking tools (important when working in an environment where a spark might create a fire or an explosion).

Because beryllium is a hard, tough metal, beryllium alloys are used for high-speed aircraft, missiles, and spacecraft such as the space shuttle. Beryllium oxide has a very high melting point, so it is useful in situations where resistance to high temperatures is important, such as in nuclear reactors as well as in ceramic applications. Because beryllium is virtually transparent to X-rays, it is used as a "window" in X-ray machines.

Natural beryllium crystals are beautiful. They include such familiar gems as emeralds and aquamarines. Beryllium and its compounds are not only extremely poisonous, but they are **carcinogenic** as well.

Atomic weight: 9.01
Melting point: approximately 2332°F (1277.85°C)

#5

Boron

B

Discovery: Discovered simultaneously by Joseph-Louis Gay-Lussac and Louis-Jacques Thenard in Paris, and Sir Humphry Davy in London in 1808

Origin of name: Boron gets its name from borax, the principal ore in which it is found.

Boron, a brittle, nonmetallic element, is usually found as a gray powder. In its pure state, it is a brown, diamond-hard crystal. It never occurs in its pure state in nature but can be found in some volcanic spring waters as well as in the form of borates in minerals such as borax (a compound of boron, water, and sodium). The most important sources of boron are borax, which is found in extensive deposits in Turkey, and the mineral rasorite, which is found in California's Mojave Desert. Borax is used in laundry products and as a

▲ *Boron*

water softener in areas where water contains large amounts of dissolved minerals.

Boron, which burns with a distinctive green color, is used in fireworks and in solid fuel rockets as an igniter. One of the most important compounds of boron is boric acid, which is used widely as a mild antiseptic. Boron is also used in the manufacture of heat-resistant borosilicate glass. Cookware made of Pyrex, which is a borosilicate glass, can be found in most kitchens.

Boron is an essential mineral for plants and is an important part of most plant foods. Some of its compounds show promise in treating arthritis. While generally non-poisonous, an accumulation of boron in the body can be toxic.

Atomic weight: 10.8
Melting point: 4171.73°F (2299.85°C)

#6

Carbon

C

Discovery: Known since ancient times.

Origin of name: It gets its name from *carbos,* the Greek word for "charcoal."

Known since ancient times, carbon is found throughout the universe and is one of the most important elements in biology. The primary reason for carbon's importance is that it readily makes long chains of mole-

The Lore of the Elements

cules by linking up with other carbon atoms. These chains form a central core to which other elements can attach, allowing complex molecules such as DNA to form. In fact, carbon is such an essential part of the DNA molecule that life as we know it on Earth is often referred to as "carbon-based life." Virtually any molecule containing carbon is called an "organic molecule" whether it is directly related to some life form or not. Carbon forms molecules so readily that there are more than 2 million known carbon-based organic molecules, one and a half times as many compounds as those formed by all of the other elements combined.

Carbon is found naturally in three forms that are so different from one another that it is hard to believe they are the same element: diamond, graphite, and coal. (Radically different forms of an element are called **allotropes**.) While all three are composed of nothing but carbon atoms, these atoms are arranged very differently in each substance. Graphite is so slippery that it is often used as a lubricant. Its carbon atoms are bound in very thin layers—much like a stack of playing cards. The carbon atoms are tightly bonded in two directions, but very weakly between layers. A familiar use for graphite is the "lead" in a pencil. A diamond, on the other hand, achieves its remarkable hardness because its carbon atoms are linked in a tight, cubical crystal pattern that is enormously strong, as though the stack of playing cards had all been glued together.

A third form of carbon can be found in coal, which contains noncrystalline carbon. Anthracite coal is about 80 percent carbon and bituminous coal contains about 40 to 50 percent. The burning of coal and other

▲ *Carbon can be found in three common forms: coal, graphite, and diamond (shown here in both its natural crystal form and as a cut gem).*

fuels that contain carbon creates carbon dioxide, a greenhouse gas. A greenhouse gas is one that helps trap the Sun's heat, in much the same way that the glass panels of a greenhouse trap the warmth of the Sun inside. Increased levels of carbon dioxide in Earth's atmosphere, many scientists believe, may be causing the average temperature of Earth to rise. If true, this could cause great problems in weather, sea level changes, and agriculture.

Recently, an entirely new, fourth form of carbon was discovered. In it, sixty atoms of carbon are arranged in a hollow sphere. Because they resemble the geodesic domes developed by inventor Buckminster Fuller, the new form of carbon has been named buckminsterfullerite or fullerene, but most call the molecules "buckyballs" for short. Sometimes, fullerine molecules take the form of hollow tubes with rounded ends. These are called "buckytubes."

Research has only just begun on practical applications for fullerene. Some scientists believe that buckyballs and buckytubes may replace silicon as the building blocks for future electronic devices in computers and communication devices. Buckytubes are among the strongest materials known and are already finding practical use in composite materials and as surface coatings to improve wear resistance. Because buckyballs are hollow and can contain molecules of other substances, they may find application in drug delivery systems.

Atomic weight: 12
Melting point: 6416.33°C (3546.85°C)

▲ *Nitrogen is a vital component of fertilizers.*

#7
Nitrogen
N

Discovery: Daniel Rutherford in 1772; recognized as an element in 1776

Origin of name: The name comes from the Greek words *nitron genes,* which means "nitre forming." Nitre is an old word for the compound now called potassium nitrate, or saltpeter.

Nitrogen is a colorless, odorless gas that forms 78 percent of Earth's atmosphere. It is an essential part of DNA and one of the building blocks of protein, so it is an important part of our diet. There is a complex "nitrogen cycle" in nature, in which nitrogen can be tracked as it is passed from the air to plants, from plants to animals, and from animals to the soil. From there it can be recycled or washed into rivers where microbes convert it back into nitrogen gas and return it to the atmosphere. About 55 million tons (50 million metric tons) of nitrogen are extracted from the atmosphere every year. It is used mainly in making fertilizer, as well as in making plastics, dyes, and explosives. Liquid nitrogen is used as a refrigerant. Nitrogen is such an inert gas (Lavoisier wanted to call it azote, which means "lifeless") that it is often used to protect very delicate materials from corrosion or deterioration.

Atomic weight: 14
Melting point: −345.75°F (−209.86°C)

#8

Oxygen

O

Discovery: Discovered independently in 1774 by Joseph Priestley in England and C. W. Scheele in Sweden

Origin of name: Its name comes from the Greek word *oxygenes,* meaning "acid producing."

Oxygen is a colorless, odorless gas that makes up 21 percent of Earth's atmosphere and 46 percent of Earth's crust. It is, in fact, one of the most abundant elements on our planet. It is also an essential part of life on our planet. Not only do we need oxygen to breathe, but it is, like nitrogen and carbon, an essential part of protein and DNA.

Oxygen is a highly **reactive** gas that readily—and sometimes even enthusiastically—combines with most of the other elements as well as most compounds. This process is called oxidation. All of the water on Earth, for instance, is the result of the oxidation of hydrogen. When oxygen combines with other elements, heat is released. We've all seen this when things burn: The heat you feel is the result of oxidation. The warmth of your body is also the result of oxidation as your body "burns" the food you eat.

Most free oxygen in the atmosphere is in the form of a molecule composed of two oxygen atoms—O_2. Another form is a blue gas called **ozone**. Molecules of ozone consist of three oxygen atoms—O_3. Unlike normal oxygen, ozone is highly corrosive and poisonous. Much of the ozone in our atmosphere is the result of the electrical energy of lightning, which creates ozone molecules from oxygen molecules. The distinctive smell you can detect after an electrical storm, or around electric motors, is ozone. Ozone, however, is vital to life on Earth. A layer of the gas high in Earth's atmosphere filters out ultraviolet radiation from the Sun that could be harmful to most life forms.

Atomic weight: 15.99
Melting point: −361.08°F (−218.35°C)

#9

Fluorine

F

Discovery: Henri Moissan in 1886

Origin of name: It comes from the Latin word *fleure,* which means "to flow."

Fluorine is part of the group of elements known as the **halogens**, or "salt formers." It is a pale greenish-yellow gas that is too reactive to be found in nature, but is instead always found in combination with other elements. It is found naturally in many minerals such as cryolite and fluorspar,

◄ *Fluorite is a mineral containing fluorine.*

from which thousands of tons of fluorine are extracted every year.

Fluorine is the most reactive element ever discovered. In concentrated form it will burn steel, gold, copper, chromium, silver, lead, and platinum. It will even burn asbestos, glass, and water! Fluorine's discoverer, French scientist Henri Moissan, was nearly killed by its vapors, but he survived to win a Nobel Prize in Chemistry for his discovery. Research into fluorine's properties was hampered for many decades because of the dangers in handling it. After all, how do you keep something that will burn, eat, or corrode just about anything a container might be made of, including glass, steel, and plastic?

World War II research into the development of the atomic bomb spurred new interest in fluorine. It was discovered that it could be used to turn uranium into a gas, which made it easier to separate fissionable uranium-235 from ordinary uranium-238. This required vast quantities of fluorine, which in turn required research into just how to handle the element (it can be kept in containers made of nickel or an alloy called Monel).

While fluorine is about as dangerous a substance as can be imagined, fluorine compounds are among the most useful ever discovered. Many of these are beneficial to good health and form the basis for many antibiotics. Since very small amounts of fluorine can help prevent tooth decay, many cities add sodium fluoride to public drinking water supplies. Many toothpastes contain this same compound. Ironically, many **fluorocarbons** (compounds of fluorine and carbon) make excellent fire-extinguishing and fire-retardant materials. The familiar Teflon coating on kitchen pots and pans is a fluorocarbon.

Other fluorine-containing molecules have not proved so benign. Chlorofluorocarbons (CFCs) are a variety of different gases that are composed of atoms of chlorine, fluorine, and carbon. They were once widely used as the propellant in aerosol cans. Although generally harmless to humans, it was discovered that CFCs could deplete the layer of ozone (a form of oxygen) that lies high in Earth's atmosphere. Theory suggests that when CFCs reach the altitude of the ozone layer, ultraviolet light from the Sun breaks down the CFC molecule. This releases the chlorine, which breaks down the ozone molecule. Because ozone prevents dangerous ultraviolet light from the Sun from reaching the surface of Earth, this became a serious concern, especially when a large "hole" was discovered in the ozone layer. Many countries, including the United States, have banned the use of CFCs.

Studies of animals suggest that fluorine might be an essential element for human health, though this has not yet been proven. Because of this, dietary sources for fluorine have not been established, though saltwater fish such as salmon, halibut, and orange roughy are good animal sources of the element.

Atomic weight: 18.99
Melting point: −362.47°F (−219.15°C)

#10

Neon
Ne

Discovery: Sir William Ramsay and M. W. Travers in 1898

Origin of name: Its name comes from the Greek word *neos,* which means "new."

Neon is a colorless, odorless gas. It is an utterly inert substance that will not combine with any other element or substance. Because of this, it is neither toxic nor does it have any biological role. It exists naturally in Earth's atmosphere, but in very small quantities—only about 0.002 percent of the atmosphere is neon. Because it glows a beautiful orange-red when an electrical current is passed through it, neon is used in the lighting fixtures that have been named after the gas. (Although all signs like this are commonly referred to as "neon signs," only the orange-glowing ones use neon gas. Other colors are created by using different gases.) Commercial quantities of neon are produced as a by-product of the manufacture of liquified air.

Atomic weight: 20.17
Melting point: −415.61°F (−248.67°C)

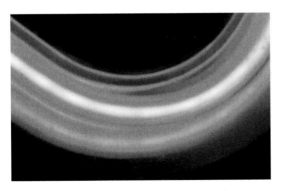

▲ *Neon gives off its typical glow when an electric current passes through it.*

#11

Sodium
Na

Discovery: Sir Humphry Davy in 1807

Origin of name: It is named for "soda"; the chemical symbol, Na, is derived from the Latin word for soda, *natrium.*

Sodium is a soft, silvery metal that is so light it will float on water. This is not a very good thing to try, however, since sodium reacts violently with water. If enough of the metal is exposed to water, it will ignite. To be stored safely, sodium usually has to be coated with wax to isolate it from air and moisture. Sodium is so soft it can be cut with a knife.

The sixth most abundant element on Earth, sodium is never found in nature because it is so reactive. There are few uses for the metal itself—liquid sodium is used in the heat exchangers of nuclear reactors—instead, it is usually employed in the form of one of its many compounds. Ordinary table salt, for instance, is sodium chloride, and baking soda is sodium bicarbonate. Energy efficient sodium-vapor lights are used to illuminate parking lots and other large areas. They are recognizable by the yellow light they produce, the characteristic color of sodium's spectrum.

Sodium is one of the essential minerals we need to maintain good health. It helps regulate the fluid levels in our bodies. Since we steadily lose the sodium in our bodies, we have to constantly replace it. We need only about 3 grams a day, mostly from the salt we eat, but most people consume far more sodium than they really need. Although it is considered nontoxic, too much salt can lead to high blood pressure and other problems.

Atomic weight: 22.98
Melting point: 208.06°F (97.81°C)

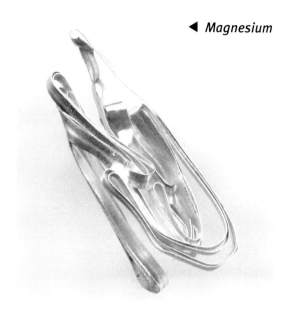

◀ *Magnesium*

#12
Magnesium
Mg

Discovery: First recognized as an element by Joseph Black in 1755, though it was not isolated until 1808 by Sir Humphry Davy.

Origin of name: It is named in honor of Magnesia, a region of Greece where it was first found.

Magnesium is a soft, silvery-white metal that burns with an intensely brilliant white light. For this reason one of its first uses was in the flash powder photographers used to illuminate their subjects before the invention of the flashbulb (which has now been replaced by the strobe light). Magnesium is still employed in flares that are used to illuminate large areas. Magnesium is a very lightweight metal, only one third as dense as aluminum. Because it easily reacts with oxygen, it is usually mixed with other metals in making strong, lightweight, corrosion-resistant alloys. These alloys are used in making bicycle frames, automobiles, and aircraft parts.

Magnesium is the eighth most abundant element on Earth, though it is never found in its free form. Vast amounts of magnesium are dissolved in Earth's oceans, so most commercial magnesium is extracted from seawater. It is an essential element for good health, though we need very little of it: only about 250–350 milligrams a day. Among other things, it is used in building bones, making proteins, regulating body temperature, and helping to hold the calcium in tooth enamel. We get most of what we need from wheat bran, whole grains, leafy green vegetables, meat, milk, nuts, beans, bananas, and apricots. Milk of magnesia (magnesium hydroxide), Epsom salts (magnesium sulfate), magnesium chloride, and magnesium citrate are used for medicinal purposes.

Atomic weight: 24.3
Melting point: 1199.93°F (648.85°C)

#13
Aluminum
Al

Discovery: Discovered in an impure form by Danish scientist Hans Oersted in 1825, and isolated as an element in 1827 by Friedrich Wöhler

Origin of name: The name comes from the Latin word *alumen,* for the mineral alum.

Aluminum, a light, silvery metal, is the most abundant of all the metals, forming more than 8 percent of Earth's crust. It is lightweight, hard, strong, and does not rust. Iron and steel are gradually destroyed as oxidation turns their surfaces to rust. Aluminum, on the other hand, forms a film of aluminum oxide that actually protects it from air and water. It is used widely in the manufacture of thousands of products, from aircraft to automobile engines to soft drink cans. Since pure aluminum is soft, it is often combined with other metals, such as copper or magnesium, when it is to be used in construction. Corundum—aluminum oxide—is one of the hardest substances known. It is used to grind and polish metal and glass.

We are so used to aluminum being so cheap—we think nothing of throwing away millions of cans and miles of aluminum foil—that it is hard to believe that in the nineteenth century a pound could cost over five hundred dollars! This is because it was once very difficult and expensive to obtain the pure metal. It was not until the invention of the electrolytic process that aluminum became cheap enough to use commercially. This process extracts the metal from its oxide by passing a powerful electric current through the compound. It still requires a great deal of power to extract the metal, but aluminum has so many uses and is so easy to recycle, that it is worthwhile.

Because aluminum conducts electricity well and is so lightweight, it is often used in high-voltage transmission lines. Aluminum is also a good reflector of radiation. The mirrors in most reflecting telescopes consist of

▲ *Aluminum*

Aluminum is obtained from an ore called ▶
bauxite, which is seen here spilling from
chutes into a freight car.

glass with a thin film of aluminum on the surface.

Aluminum has no role in our health. Though it has been suggested that there may be a link between aluminum and Alzheimer's disease, the metal is considered to be nontoxic.

Atomic weight: 26.98
Melting point: approximately 1219.73°F
(959.85°C)

#14
Silicon
Si

Discovery: Jöns Jakob Berzelius in 1824

Origin of name: It is named from
silicus, **the Latin word for flint.**

Silicon in pure form is a brown powder, but when crystallized it is a metallic gray. Next to oxygen, it is the most abundant element on Earth, forming more than 25 percent of the planet's crust. It never appears free, but always in combination with other elements, primarily oxygen. Sand, quartz, and flint are silicon dioxide, the most important form of silicon, as are many gems such as opals, amethyst, and agates. Silicon also appears in the form of silicates, such as asbestos,

clay, and mica. It is probably most familiar, however, as the silicon chip used in the semiconductors at the heart of computers and other electronic devices. So important is the silicon chip that one of the main manufacturing regions in California has been nicknamed "Silicon Valley."

Silicon had, and still has, uses other than in electronics. Sand is the primary constituent of glass, and clay is the basis for the ceramics industry. Silicon carbide is an important abrasive. A wide variety of products—from lubricants to rubberlike materials—are made from silicones, long

▲ *Here, silicon is*
in the form of a dark
gray powder.

The Lore of the Elements

molecules that are prepared from organic silicon compounds. One familiar type of silicone is Silly Putty. A silicone gel was also used in breast implants because it created a very natural appearance. Fear that silicone leaking from the implants might be causing health problems has resulted in the near-abandonment of its use, although scientists and doctors never found any evidence that silicone caused any harm.

Silicon is an essential element for plant and animal life. It helps maintain the health of our connective tissue and skin. We need only extremely small amounts (2 to 5 milligrams a day), so we get all that we need from plants and grains such as oats, barley, and rice. Silicon itself is nontoxic, but many of the silicates are carcinogenic.

Atomic weight: 28.08
Melting point: 2569.73°F (1409.85°C)

#15
Phosphorus
P

Discovery: Hennig Brandt in 1669

Origin of name: The name comes from the Greek word *phosphoros*, which means "bringer of light," because it glows in the dark.

There are two very different forms, or allotropes, of phosphorus, with very different characteristics. White phosphorus glows in the dark and will spontaneously ignite when exposed to air above 86°F (30°C). It is also a deadly poison and can cause severe burns if it contacts the skin. In spite of its name, white phosphorus is a pale yellow, waxy substance, and in its pure form it is transparent. Red phosphorus, a powder made by heating white phosphorus to about 486°F (250°C) in a vacuum, does not glow in the dark, does not spontaneously ignite, and is not poisonous.

Phosphorus, which is not found free in nature, has many important industrial applications. Red phosphorus is used in the manufacture of pesticides. Because it does not ignite spontaneously, it is used in making safety matches. The rough surface on the outside of a book or box of matches is phosphorus combined with ground glass.

One of the most important uses of phosphorus is in the manufacture of phosphates for fertilizers. Phosphorus is such an important ingredient of plant life that phosphorus-poor soil is barren. Phosphorus is also used in some detergents, though this use has caused some alarm among ecologists. When phosphates wash into rivers and lakes, they encourage the growth of algae, which in turn robs the water of oxygen, causing much harm to fish and other aquatic animals. Because of this problem, most detergents today are made without phosphates.

Phosphorus is part of the DNA molecule, so it would be essential to life even if there were not many phosphorus compounds our bodies also need. Only about 1 percent of your body weight is phosphorus, 85 percent of which is in your bones, which are mainly calcium phosphate, a combination of calcium and phosphorus. Phosphorus helps build strong bones and teeth, helps in the release of energy from the food you eat, and is an essential part of DNA. Most of the phosphorus you need comes from fish, meat, poultry, dairy products, eggs, peas, beans, and nuts.

Atomic weight: 30.97
Melting point: approximately 111.65°F (44.25°C) for white phosphorus, approximately 769.73°F (409.85°C) for red phosphorus

#16
Sulfur
S

Discovery: Known since ancient times

Origin of name: It comes from the Latin name for the element.

▲ *Sulfur is one of the three traditional ingredients in the gunpowder used in making fireworks.*

Sulfur occurs naturally as pale yellow, brittle crystals. It burns easily with a blue flame, creating an unpleasant, acrid odor like that of rotten eggs, caused by the formation of the gas hydrogen sulfide. Because it burns

◀ *Sulfur*

so readily, it was known as brimstone in Old English, which means "stone that burns," and it is still sometimes called by that name. Sulfur compounds are found widely throughout nature. Among these are iron pyrite (known more famously as fool's gold), plaster of paris (gypsum), and Epsom salts (hydrated magnesium sulfate, a laxative).

Sulfur's most important use is in the manufacture of sulfuric acid, and most of the sulfur that is mined goes into its production. Sulfur is also one of the three classic ingredients of gunpowder (the other two are saltpeter and charcoal). Coal and oil contain sulfur, and when they are burned, sulfur dioxide is formed. This is converted into sulfuric acid in the atmosphere and is the primary source of "acid rain," an environmental problem in industrial areas.

The Lore of the Elements

◀ *Huge mounds of sulfur await shipment at a mine in Vancouver, British Columbia.*

Nontoxic in its elemental form (though many sulfur compounds are poisonous), sulfur is an essential element in our good health, for which we need about 1 gram a day. We get this from foods such as fish, meat, eggs, and milk. Our body uses it in the formation of fats and bones.

Atomic weight: 32.06
Melting point: 235.13°F (112.85°C)

#17
Chlorine
Cl

Discovery: Carl Wilhelm Scheele in 1774; it was Sir Humphry Davy, however, who recognized it as an element in 1810 and named it

Origin of name: The name comes from *chloros,* the Greek word for "yellow-green."

Chlorine is a dense, yellowish green gas with a distinctive, sharp smell. It is so poisonous that it was once used as a weapon in World War I, when the Germans released large quantities of the gas on Allied armies. Although it is highly toxic, it is one of the two elements that form common table salt, otherwise known as sodium chloride. Dangerous though chlorine may be, it is useful in manufacturing many substances, such as laundry bleach, antiseptics, insecticides, and PVC (polyvinyl chloride) plastic. Important chlorine compounds include chloroform (an anesthetic) and carbon tetrachloride (a cleaning fluid). Chlorine is used to purify the water in drinking supplies and swimming pools. Chlorine is produced commercially from salt.

One of the most important chlorine products is hydrochloric acid. About 3 million tons are produced every year. It is used to etch glass and to remove rust from steel. Hydrochloric acid is also the acid produced by the stomach, where it breaks down proteins so they can be digested. Chlorine helps keep the acids in your body in balance. You get all you need from the salt you eat.

Atomic weight: 35.45
Melting point: −150.07°F (−101.15°C)

#18

Argon

Ar

Discovery: Lord Rayleigh and Sir William Ramsay in 1894

Origin of name: It comes from the Greek word *argos*, which means "inactive."

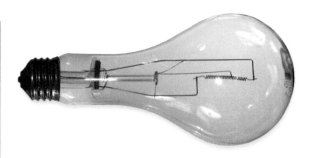

▲ *Argon is used in lightbulbs to protect the filament.*

Argon is one of the inert gases—a group that also includes helium and neon, among others. It is colorless, odorless, and does not combine naturally with any other element. It forms about 1 percent of Earth's atmosphere, making it the third most abundant gas, after nitrogen and oxygen.

None of the inert gases (which are sometimes called the noble gases because they seem to stand aloof from all the other elements, as though they were royalty) were known at the time Mendeleyev created his table of the elements, so no provision was made for them. The discovery of argon in 1894 dictated the creation of a new column. Argon was later joined by krypton, helium, neon, xenon, and radon.

The primary use for argon is in the manufacture of lightbulbs. Because it is inert, it does not corrode the metal filament, as oxygen would, while at the same time it helps carry away some of the heat. For these reasons it makes the filament last much longer. It is also used by welders, who shield their work with it to prevent it from burning. It is

manufactured by extracting it from liquified air.

Since argon is totally inert, it is neither toxic nor has any known biological function.

Atomic weight: 39.94
Melting point: −308.47°F (−189.15°C)

#19

Potassium

K

Discovery: Sir Humphry Davy in 1807

Origin of name: The name is taken from that of potash, the compound from which Davy first isolated the element. The chemical symbol, K, is from *kalium*, the Latin word for potash.

Potassium is a soft, silvery metal, one of the least dense of all the metals and seventh most abundant on Earth. Like its cousins lithium and sodium, it oxidizes

The Lore of the Elements

rapidly. It will react violently with water to release hydrogen, which then burns spontaneously. As might be expected, potassium is not found free in nature. Because it is so reactive it must be kept stored in mineral oil.

Potassium is vital to plant life; therefore most potassium, which is mined in the form of potassium chloride, is used in the manufacture of fertilizers.

Your heart, nerves, and muscles need potassium, and you need to consume about 7 grams a day to stay healthy. You can get the potassium you need from foods such as wheat bran, whole grains, leafy green vegetables, meat, milk, nuts, beans, bananas, and apricots.

Atomic weight: 39.09
Melting point: 145.13°F (62.85°C)

#20
Calcium
Ca

Discovery: Sir Humphry Davy in 1808

Origin of name: It comes from *calx*, the Latin word for lime, of which calcium is one of the main components.

Calcium is a soft, silvery-white metal that, like its relatives sodium and potassium, reacts with water. It is one of the most abundant elements on Earth, composing some 3 percent of Earth's crust. It is not

Calcium stored ▶
in mineral oil

found free in nature, but always in combination with other elements. Some natural forms of calcium include gypsum (calcium sulfate, which is used to make plaster of paris) and limestone (calcium carbonate). There are vast deposits of limestone all over the world. Much of these are the remains of ancient shellfish, which made their shells—as do modern clams and oysters—from calcium carbonate. When limestone is heated, it gives off carbon dioxide gas, leaving behind calcium oxide (quicklime). Known and used since ancient times, this has many commercial uses: in manufacturing cement, for example, and in water softeners, where it helps remove minerals dissolved in the water. Calcium carbonate neutralizes acids, so it is one of the main ingredients in the antacids that people take for upset stomachs.

▲ *Limestone (calcium carbonate)*

Calcium is essential to your good health. Your bones and teeth, especially, are made mostly of calcium phosphate. It also helps to regulate your heartbeat. Your body contains about 2.2 pounds (1 kilogram) of calcium. Milk and dairy products are the richest source of calcium.

Atomic weight: 40.07
Melting point: 1541.93°F (838.85°C)

#21
Scandium
Sc

Discovery: Lars Frederik Nilson in 1879

Origin of name: Nilson named it for his native Sweden (using the Latin name Scandia).

Predicted by Mendeleyev's table, scandium is a silvery metal that tarnishes fairly easily, although it is resistant to corrosion. A scarce metal (more scandium is found in the Sun and other stars than on Earth), it has very few commercial applications. One of these is in the manufacture of electric lights that closely approximate natural sunlight. These have found use in illuminating night football and baseball games. Since it is almost as light as aluminum and has a much higher melting point, scandium may have some future use in spacecraft, where light weight combined with resistance to high temperatures is important. Scandium has no known biological function, but it may be a carcinogen.

Atomic weight: 44.95
Melting point: 2805.53°F (1540.85°C)

#22
Titanium
Ti

Discovery: Rev. William Gregor in 1791; isolated by Jöns Jakob Berzelius in 1825. The pure metal itself was not made until 1910.

Origin of name: It is named after the Titans, who in Greek mythology were the sons of Uranus, the god of the sky, and Gaia, the goddess of Earth.

Titanium is a hard, silvery metal that is stronger and lighter than steel. It is also highly resistant to corrosion and metal fatigue (stresses caused by flexing and bending). It is widely used in the aerospace industry in the form of many different lightweight alloys with aluminum, molybdenum,

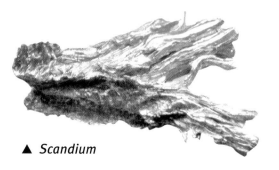

▲ *Scandium*

#23
Vanadium
V

Discovery: Andres Manuel del Rio in 1801

Origin of name: It is named after Vanadis, a Norse name for the Scandinavian goddess Freyja, because of the many different-colored compounds the element can form.

▲ *Lightweight, strong, heat-resistant titanium is important in the manufacture of aircraft, such as this supersonic jet.*

and iron. Not only are these strong, but they are also capable of resisting very high temperatures and for this reason many titanium alloys are used in the manufacture of jet engines. Titanium dioxide is a brilliant white substance that is used in the manufacture of excellent white paints for both house painters and artists. It not only does a beautiful white, but is also a good reflector of infrared radiation from the Sun. Titanium has no known biological function, though it may be a carcinogen.

Atomic weight: 47.88
Melting point: 3019.73°F (1659.85°C)

Although vanadium was discovered in Mexico City by del Rio in 1801, a French chemist convinced him that what he had discovered was only impure chromium. The element was not rediscovered until 1830 by Nils Gabriel Sefström, who gave it its name.

Vanadium is a soft, silvery metal that is highly resistant to corrosion. It is used in many different alloys, including steel, where it creates tough, high-temperature–resistant metals that are used for armor plating, axles, and piston rods. As little as 1 percent each of vanadium and chromium added to steel will make it resistant to shock and vibration.

Although our bodies contain extremely small amounts of vanadium—between 0.1 and 1 milligram—it is not clear yet how, or even if, our bodies use it. Some researchers suspect that it may help our bodies process iodine and aid in the functioning of our thyroid gland. Vanadium is found in foods such as parsley, black pepper, mushrooms, and shellfish.

Atomic weight: 50.94
Melting point: approximately 3428.33°F (1886.85°C)

Titanium ▶
jewelry

#24

Chromium
Cr

Discovery: N. L. Vauquelin in 1797

Origin of name: It is named from *chroma*, the Greek word for "color," for the many-colored compounds it can form.

Chromium is a hard, silvery-blue metal. When exposed to air, a thin, invisible coating is formed that makes the metal resistant to corrosion. It is this quality that makes chromium so highly desirable for plating (or coating) other metals to protect them from corrosion. Because it can take a high, mirrorlike polish, many things are chromium-plated for purely decorative reasons.

Chromium is added to steel to not only make it harder but also to make it corrosion-resistant, or "stainless." Chromium compounds can be very colorful, and many of them are used in paints. Chromium oxide, for instance, is bright green, while lead chromate is yellow. Rubies get their color from chromium, as does emerald-green glass.

It is an essential element in our bodies, where we use it to help process blood sugar. You get the chromium you need from foods such as whole grains, broccoli, turkey, grape juice, and potatoes. Too much chromium, however, can be carcinogenic, and most chromium compounds are poisonous.

Atomic weight: 51.99
Melting point: 3374.33°F (1856.85°C)

▲ *Chromium is plated on other metals to protect them and provide an attractive, silvery finish, such as on this antique automobile hood ornament.*

#25

Manganese
Mn

Discovery: J. G. Grahn in 1774

Origin of name: The name comes from *magnes*, the Latin word for "magnet."

A hard, gray metal, manganese is too brittle to be used by itself. But when added to steel, it makes the metal much harder while allowing it to still remain flexible. When mixed with aluminum and antimony, it forms highly magnetic alloys. It is also a necessary element for living things. An important compound of manganese is potassium permanganate. When dissolved in water, potassium permanganate makes a dark purple solution. When an acid is added, however, the solution becomes light pink. Scientists use this trait as an indicator of the presence of acids in substances. Potassium permanganate is also used to absorb toxic gases and in water purification systems.

Manganese is obtained from mines in South Africa and India as well as from strange, spherical nodules found on the ocean floor. These were probably created by microorganisms that have the ability to extract the manganese that is dissolved in the surrounding water.

Your body contains about 0.0004 ounce (0.011 gram) of manganese. Without manganese, your bones would lose their hardness, become spongy, and break more easily. It activates many enzymes and helps your body make use of vitamin B. You get manganese from foods like wheat germ, nuts, whole grains, oysters, sweet potatoes, tofu, chocolate, brewed tea, and dark molasses.

Atomic weight: 54.93
Melting point: 2270.93°F (1243.85°C)

Manganese ▶

#26

Iron

Fe

Discovery: Known since ancient times

Origin of name: The name comes from an old Anglo-Saxon word. Iron derives its symbol, Fe, from *ferrum*, the Latin word for "iron."

Iron, a silvery metal that quickly corrodes when exposed to moist air, is the most abundant, cheapest, and most important of all the metals, with worldwide production exceeding 771,618,000 tons (700 million metric tons) every year. Iron was one of the first metals used by early humans because it is relatively soft and can be easily worked and shaped into tools and weapons. Even today, iron accounts for 90 percent of all the metal that is mined. Iron is the fourth most abundant element in Earth's crust, and the core of our planet may be a huge mass of iron.

Iron is never found in its pure state, but always in combination with other elements, usually with oxygen. Two of the most important ores that are mined for their iron are hematite and magnetite. The oxygen is removed by melting the ore and adding carbon. The carbon combines with the oxygen, leaving behind the pure metal.

Because pure iron is somewhat brittle, a small amount of carbon is added to create the much harder, durable steel. Wrought iron has very little carbon added, so that it can remain easily worked. It is commonly used to make decorative architectural objects such as fences and railings. If chromium is then added, rustproof stainless steel is formed. Combinations of other elements can also be added, each contributing their special characteristics.

Iron or iron alloys are used everywhere. Cast iron is used to make gasoline and diesel engine blocks and wood-burning stoves. Galvanized iron (iron coated with zinc) is used in roofing and automobile bodies. Steel is used wherever great strength and durability are important, such as in construction, shipbuilding, automobiles, machinery, cans, and household appliances. Because stainless steel does not rust, it is used in making surgical instruments, hospital and food-handling equipment, cutlery, and other applications where cleanliness is important. Extremely hard steel alloyed with tungsten, chromium, and other elements is used in making tools and drill bits.

Iron is absolutely essential to your health, where iron's affinity for oxygen is vital. Most of the 0.14 ounce (4 grams) of iron in your body is in the hemoglobin in your blood, which carries oxygen from your lungs. You need at least 0.0003 ounce (0.0085 gram) in your diet every day to remain healthy. You can get iron from green vegetables, meats, and fish.

Atomic weight: 55.84
Melting point: 2794.73°F (1534.85°C)

▲ *A vast open-pit iron mine in Michigan*

#27

Cobalt

Co

Discovery: G. Brandt in 1735

Origin of name: It derives from the German word *kobald,* which means "goblin." The reason for choosing this name is obscure, but it may have come from miners who attributed accidents to evil spirits or goblins.

Cobalt is a silvery-blue metal that can be magnetized. It is used in the production of pigments for paint, especially in creating the beautiful blue known as cobalt blue. The same ability to produce brilliant blue colors also makes cobalt useful in the production of ceramics and glass. Because it is very resistant to corrosion, and also provides a beautiful, lustrous finish, it is used to plate (coat) other materials. As an alloy with iron, nickel, and other metals, where it adds resistance to corrosion, it is used in jet turbines.

Since it is easily magnetized and retains its magnetism at high temperatures, a quarter of the cobalt mined today is used in the manufacture of the powerful magnetic alloy called alnico, a combination of aluminum, nickel, and cobalt.

As a part of vitamin B-12, it is an essential element for a healthy body. You get what you need from dairy products, meat,

Cobalt ▶

and green leafy vegetables. The radioactive isotope, cobalt-60, is used in the treatment of cancer.

Atomic weight: 58.93
Melting point: 2722.73°F
(1494.85°C)

#28

Nickel

Ni

Discovery: Axel Frederik Cronstedt in 1751

Origin of name: From the German word for Satan (derived from a shortened form of the German word *Kupfernickel,* which means "Devil's copper" or "St. Nicholas's copper").

Nickel is a silvery metal that composes 25 percent of the U.S. five-cent coin. Although the rest of the coin is copper, the nickname

Most meteorites, like this one found in the Willamette Valley of Oregon, are made of nickel and iron.

"nickel" has stuck. About 30 percent of the world's nickel is found in Sudbury, Ontario, Canada. Much of this is mined from the remnants of an asteroid that crashed into the Earth many millions of years ago.

Nickel resists corrosion even at high temperatures. For this reason it is used in gas turbines and rocket engines. It is also one of the elements added to some stainless steels, and nickel plating is used to protect the surfaces of other metals. The nichrome wire used in electric toasters and heaters is an alloy of nickel and chrome. Another important alloy is monel, a hard, corrosion-resistant combination of nickel and copper. Nickel is also important in the manufacture of rechargeable nickel-cadmium (NiCad) batteries.

Some nickel compounds can cause cancer if the dust is inhaled, and some individuals are allergic to contact with the metal. Nickel cannot be entirely avoided because we take in some nickel compounds with our diet, where it is usually found in whole grains and vegetables.

Atomic weight: 58
Melting point: 2647°F (1453°C)

#29
Copper
Cu

Discovery: Known since ancient times

Origin of name: It derives its name and symbol, Cu, from Cuprum, the Latin name for the island of Cyprus, where copper was mined by the Romans.

Although a somewhat rare element, copper has been mined and worked for at least 11,000 years. Although too soft to make useful tools or weapons, it was very early discovered that it could be mixed with tin to make bronze, a much harder metal that could be made into coins, statues, and swords. In addition to bronze, another important alloy of copper is brass, a mixture of copper and zinc. Because of its rich, golden color, it is used mainly to make decorative objects and household items such as hinges and doorknobs. Because it is also wear-resistant and a good conductor of electricity, it is often used in making switches and contacts.

Copper is a beautiful, reddish metal that can be worked easily. It is ductile, which means that it can be drawn out into very thin wires. It conducts both heat and electricity very well. Most of the copper that is produced today goes into making electrical equipment. Copper does not rust or corrode like iron and steel do. Instead, like aluminum, it forms a patina, or thin coating, of copper carbonate that protects it from the atmosphere. It is the patina that gives the metal its bright green color when exposed to the air. Although copper can be found in its natural state, it is usually found combined with other elements in the form of minerals.

One of the most useful of all metals, copper can be found everywhere in your life, from the pennies in your pocket (which are actually copper-plated zinc) to the wires in your electronic equipment to the water pipes in your house.

Copper is one of the elements that is essential to our health, though too much can be toxic (mariners used to cover the bottoms of their ships with copper plates to ward off barnacles and shipworms; today, boat hulls are often coated with copper-bearing paints for the same purpose). Your body uses copper in making many different enzymes. You get all the copper you need from foods such as organ meats, seafood, nuts, whole grains, beans, chocolate, cherries, dried fruits, milk, tea, chicken, and potatoes.

Atomic weight: 63.54
Melting point: 1982.93°F (1083.85°C)

▲ *A natural copper nugget*

#30
Zinc
Zn

Discovery: Known since ancient times
Origin of name: It comes from *zink,* the German word for the metal.

The Chinese and Indians were using zinc before 1500 B.C., and the Greeks and Romans used zinc in combination with copper to make the alloy known as brass. It was discovered to be an element in 1746 when the German chemist Andrea Sigismund Marggraf isolated the pure metal.

A hard, blue-gray, brittle metal, zinc has many commercial uses. Because it is highly resistant to corrosion, it is coated onto iron or steel by an electrical process called galvanizing, which protects the original metal from rust. Metal objects can also be coated with zinc by dipping them into a bath of the molten metal. (The frostlike crystalline pattern on the surface of galvanized metal objects is the zinc coating.) It is also used in alloys and batteries.

Zinc oxide is a valuable compound that is used in many applications, such as white paint, cosmetics, pharmaceuticals, plastics, inks, photocopiers, and even sunburn ointment. Zinc sulfide will glow in the dark and is used to make luminous dials for clocks. Since it will also glow when struck by electrons, it is one of the substances used to

▲ *Zinc*

coat the inside of television tubes and computer monitors.

Zinc is an essential element for good health. In your body it helps in the manufacture of many important enzymes as well as in metabolism (turning food into energy). Zinc can be found in foods such as oysters, beef, liver, crab, seafood, poultry, nuts, whole grains, tofu, and beans.

Atomic weight: 65.39
Melting point: 787.19°F (419.55°C)

#31 Gallium Ga

Discovery: Paul-Émile Lecoq de Boisbaudran in 1875

Origin of name: It comes from Gallia, the Latin name for France, in honor of de Boisbaudran's native country.

Gallium is a silvery, extremely soft metal resembling aluminum. Its existence was predicted in 1871 by Mendeleyev, who also predicted some of the metal's characteristics. Its main use is in the making of **semiconductors** and **light-emitting diodes (LEDs)** that are used to make the glowing letters on handheld calculators and other devices. Since it has such a high boiling point, 4357.13°F (2402.85°C), it is used in making sensors for recording temperatures too high for ordinary thermometers. On the other hand, its melting point is so low that it will melt in your hand. It also has the unusual property (shared by only a few other substances) of expanding when it freezes. When coated on a sheet of glass it forms a brilliant mirror. Gallium is nontoxic and has no known biological function.

Atomic weight: 69.72
Melting point: 85.73°F (29.85°C)

#32 Germanium Ge

Discovery: C. A. Winkler in 1886

Origin of name: It was named in honor of Winkler's native country, Germany.

Predicted by Mendeleyev in 1871, germanium is a dark gray, brittle, metal-like substance that lies between the true metals and the nonmetallic elements. Since many of its properties resemble those of silicon, it is very important in the manufacture of semiconductors (such as transistors). A semiconductor lies halfway between materials that can conduct electricity and those that are insulators. Semiconductors such as the transistor replaced the large, bulky vacuum tubes used in the past, allowing the development of small, inexpensive electronic devices, such as computers.

Germanium oxide is a transparent material that has a very high index of refraction, or ability to bend light, which is valuable for making camera lenses and microscopes. Minerals containing germanium are very rare, so the element is usually obtained as a by-product of zinc and copper refining. It apparently has no biological function, though research is being done on the possibility that germanium compounds might be antibacterial.

Atomic weight: 72.61
Melting point: 1719°F (937.4°C)

Germanium ▼

#33
Arsenic
As

Discovery: Albertus Magnus in 1250

Origin of name: It comes from the Greek word *arsenikon* and the Latin word *arsenicum*, both of which refer to a yellow pigment containing the element.

Arsenic is a steel-gray, brittle substance that lies between the metals and nonmetals in the periodic table. Although best known as a poison, it was at one time widely used as a medicine. A compound containing arsenic, "Compound 606," was discovered by the German chemist Paul Ehrlich in 1910. It was the first cure for syphilis and until the development of antibiotics was the only known treatment for the disease. Because arsenic can be stored by the body until toxic levels are reached, even the tiniest amounts are potentially dangerous. For this reason, medicines containing arsenic are rarely used anymore.

Today, compounds of arsenic are used in making glass, semiconductors, LEDs, and rot-proof, pressure-treated wood. Combined with metals, it creates hard, corrosion-resistant alloys. Although arsenic can be found in the free state, it is obtained mostly from minerals with the wonderful names of mispickel, realgar, and orpiment.

It is possible that arsenic may be a necessary trace element, but it is most definitely toxic in even tiny amounts and is probably carcinogenic as well.

Atomic weight: 74.92
Melting point: 1502.33°F (816.85°C)

#34 Selenium
Se

Discovery: Jöns Jakob Berzelius in 1817

Origin of name: It was named in honor of the moon, which is called *selene* in Greek.

Selenium is a semimetallic substance that can exist in either one of two allotropic forms: a soft, silvery metal or a red, glasslike solid. Selenium is both **photovoltaic**—it can convert light directly into electricity—and **photoconductive**—its electrical resistance decreases as the light falling on it increases. That is, the stronger the light that falls on it, the more selenium resists conducting electricity. For this reason, selenium can be used in devices that respond to light, such as photoelectric cells, photocopiers, and solar electric cells. It can also convert alternating current to direct current.

It is an essential trace element in the human diet, where it may protect against heart disease and cancer, but is toxic if taken in excess. You get all you need from foods such as nuts, seafood, liver, whole grain pasta, sunflower seeds, oatmeal, eggs, and low-fat dairy products. Large amounts of selenium are carcinogenic and can also cause birth defects. Selenium deficiency has been linked to Sudden Infant Death Syndrome (SIDS). Many selenium compounds are extremely poisonous.

Atomic weight: 78.96
Melting point: 429.53°F (220.85°C)

Selenium ▶

#35 Bromine
Br

Discovery: Simultaneously by A. J. Balard in France and C. Löwig in Germany in 1826

Origin of name: It comes from *bromos,* a Greek word meaning "foul odor."

Bromine is a dark red, oily liquid with, as its name implies, a bad smell. It is very heavy—three times denser than water—and even its vapor is heavier than air. Extracted

The Lore of the Elements

from natural brine deposits, it is used in the manufacture of gasoline additives, insecticides, flame retardants, and some pharmaceuticals. Silver bromide is used in making the light-sensitive emulsion on photographic film and prints.

Bromine has no established biological role. Instead, it and many of its compounds are extremely toxic and contact with the liquid can corrode skin.

Atomic weight: 79.90
Melting point: 19°F (−7.2°C)

#36
Krypton
Kr

Discovery: Sir William Ramsay and M. W. Travers in 1898

Origin of name: From the Greek word *kryptos,* **which means "hidden." (The word** *krypton* **is probably most familiar as the name of Superman's home planet, though this is just a coincidence. The original creators of the superhero just liked the sound of the word.)**

Krypton is an extremely rare, colorless, odorless gas that is inert to every other substance except fluorine. It exists only in trace amounts in Earth's atmosphere. It is obtained as a by-product of making liquified air. It is used in neon tubes when a violet light is needed, in fluorescent light tubes, and (mixed with xenon) in the strobe lights used for photography.

Atomic weight: 83.8
Melting point: −251°F (−157.2°C)

#37
Rubidium
Rb

Discovery: Robert W. Bunsen and Gustav Kirchhoff in 1861

Origin of name: From *rubidius,* **the Latin word for "dark red" (the same word from which we get ruby). It was named for the red lines that identify the element's spectrum.**

Chemically similar to potassium, rubidium is a soft, silvery metal that ignites spontaneously on contact with air. It also reacts violently with water, giving off large quantities of hydrogen, which then ignite. For these reasons rubidium is usually stored in kerosene. The element is obtained during the process of refining lithium and cesium, since their ores usually also contain small amounts of rubidium.

Rubidium's relatively low melting point—only slightly above body heat—means that it can be liquid at room temperature. It has very few commercial uses, mainly as a "getter" in vacuum tubes, where a tiny amount of the metal will absorb stray gas molecules that would interfere with the operation of the tube.

Because it is easily ionized—given an electrical charge—it has been proposed as a fuel for spacecraft using ion engines. These work by emitting a stream of electrically charged particles that act like the exhaust of a rocket motor.

While rubidium is nontoxic, it has no known biological function. Since it is slightly radioactive, it has been used to locate tumors because rubidium will collect in tumors but not in healthy tissue.

Atomic weight: 85.47
Melting point: 102°F (38.89°C)

▲ *Strontium crystals*

#38

Strontium
Sr

Discovery: Discovered by Adair Crawford in 1790, but not recognized as an element until 1808 by Sir Humphry Davy

Origin of name: It is named after the Scottish village of Strontian, where the ore was first found.

Strontium is a soft, silvery metal that, like potassium and rubidium, burns on contact with air and reacts with water. It must be stored in mineral oil to prevent oxidation. Its most common commercial use is in the manufacture of fireworks, to which it adds a brilliant red color.

While it has no known function in our bodies, and is nontoxic, its similarity to cal-

cium can cause problems. Radioactive strontium-90—which can be released into the environment by nuclear bomb tests or nuclear power plant accidents—can be absorbed into bones, replacing the natural calcium there. The radioactive strontium can then destroy the marrow and cause cancer.

Atomic weight: 87.62
Melting point: 1407.2°F (764°C)

#39

Yttrium
Y

Discovery: Johan Gadolin in 1794

Origin of name: Like the elements ytterbium, terbium, and erbium, it was named after the Swedish town of Ytterby, where the element was mined.

Yttrium (pronounced I-tree-um) is a soft, silvery metal. If cut into small pieces, it will ignite spontaneously on contact with air. Larger pieces will form a film of yttrium oxide that protects the metal from further oxidation. It is a very rare metal on Earth, though samples brought back from the Moon revealed much larger quantities.

The main commercial use for this element is in lasers and the screens of color television sets, where it produces the color red. It is also used to add strength to aluminum and magnesium alloys. Yttrium has no known biological function. While it is nontoxic, it is suspected of being carcinogenic.

Atomic weight: 88.9
Melting point: 2773.4°F (1523°C)

#40
Zirconium
Zr

Discovery: M. H. Klaproth in 1789, isolated in 1824 by Jöns Jakob Berzelius

Origin of name: The name comes from *zargun*, the Arabic word for gold, because of the golden-yellow color of the zirconium crystal.

Zirconium is a hard, silvery metal that is highly resistant to corrosion. This feature, combined with the fact that zirconium does not absorb neutrons well, makes it useful in nuclear reactors where containers made of a zirconium alloy protect the uranium fuel pellets from direct contact with the coolant water. As zirconium oxide, an extremely hard, heat-resistant material, the metal is

used in the manufacture of ceramics, firebrick, crucibles, and abrasives. The mineral known as zircon (zirconium silicate) produces beautiful crystals closely resembling diamonds, which have been valued as gemstones since biblical times. Zirconium has no known biological function and is nontoxic.

Atomic weight: 91.22
Melting point: 3365.6°F (1852°C)

Zircon ▼

#41
Niobium
Nb

Discovery: Charles Hatchett in 1801

Origin of name: Since it is very similar to tantalum, which was named for Tantalus, niobium was named for Niobe, Tantalus's daughter. (Until 1950 the element was called columbium, from a mythological name for the United States.)

Niobium is a soft, silvery-white metal. Since it is highly resistant to corrosion, it is added

▲ *Niobium-plated jewelry*

to alloys of steel and other metals to improve their strength and resistance to high temperatures. It also has an important function in the field of high-temperature superconductivity. Superconductivity occurs when a substance carries electricity with little or no resistance. When some materials are heated, they become **superconductors**. Niobium can also withstand very large electrical currents, so it is useful in the creation of the giant electromagnets used by medical nuclear magnetic resonance imagers (NMRIs). These instruments can create images of the interior of the human body without the use of dangerous X-rays. Niobium is not toxic, nor does it have any known biological function.

Atomic weight: 92.9
Melting point: 4474.4°F (2468°C)

#42
Molybdenum
Mo

Discovery: Carl Wilhelm Scheele in 1778

Origin of name: It comes from *molybdos*, the Greek word for lead.

Molybdenum (usually just called moly) is a soft, silvery metal that is commonly produced as a gray powder. It is used in iron alloys, where it makes the resulting steel harder and tougher, for **catalysts** used in oil refining, and as an additive to lubricants, where it adds to the ability of oil to prevent wear. It is also used in places where resistance to high temperatures is required, such as in lamp filaments. Since it has the fifth highest melting point of all the metals, molybdenum's use was originally limited until a special water-cooled crucible was invented to contain the molten metal.

Molybdenum is an essential element in the human body, where it helps in the formation of uric acid, though we need only very tiny amounts, about 0.01 milligram a day. In larger quantities it can be toxic. Good sources for molybdenum are foods such as milk, dried beans, peas, nuts, eggs, liver, tomatoes, carrots, and meats.

Atomic weight: 95.94
Melting point: 4742.6°F (2617°C)

#43

Technetium

Tc

Discovery: Carlo Perrier and Emilio G. Segré in 1937

Origin of name: It comes from the Greek word *tekhnetos,* which means "artificial," since the element does not occur naturally.

Technetium, a silvery, radioactive metal, was the first element to be created artificially. It does not occur in nature because it has such a relatively short half-life: 212,000 years. All of the technetium that might have existed on Earth when our planet was first formed has therefore long since disappeared.

Technetium is also added to steel to retard corrosion, but only for special applications because the element is radioactive. Technetium has some medical applications—it can be injected into the bloodstream to help doctors obtain images of the heart.

Atomic weight: 98.91
Melting point: 3992°F (2200°C)

#44

Ruthenium

Ru

Discovery: Karl Karlovitch Klaus in 1844

Origin of name: Its name comes from the Latin word for Russia.

Ruthenium was originally discovered by the Polish chemist Jedrzej A. Sniadecki in 1807, who named it vestium after the Roman goddess Vesta. His discovery, however, was not generally accepted since he was unable to support his claim and eventually withdrew it. The element was found again in 1828 by the Russian scientist Gottfried Wilhelm Osann, who patriotically named it for his native country. Osann, however, was not credited with the discovery either, in part because he had failed to isolate the pure metal. Osann himself agreed with this and declined credit. Karl Karlovich Klaus finally discovered the pure metal in 1844. He retained the name ruthenium in honor of Osann's work.

A hard, brittle, silvery metal that can be found in the free state in nature, ruthenium is one of the rarest of all the metals. It is generally produced as a by-product of platinum refining. One of its few commercial uses is as a hardener in platinum and palladium alloys. It has no known biological function.

Atomic weight: 101.07
Melting point: 4082°F (2250°C)

#45

Rhodium
Rh

Discovery: William Hyde Wollaston in 1803

Origin of name: It comes from the Greek word *rhodon*, meaning "rose," because many compounds of rhodium are rose colored.

A hard, silvery metal, rhodium is the rarest nonradioactive metal on Earth. Only 3.3 tons (3 metric tons) are produced every year, usually during the refining of platinum. It is used in platinum alloys to add hardness and, along with platinum and palladium, in the catalytic converters that reduce pollution from automobile engines. It has no known biological function, but it is suspected of being a cancer-causing agent.

Atomic weight: 102.92
Melting point: 3570.8°F (1966°C)

▲ *Rhodium-plated jewelry*

#46

Palladium
Pd

Discovery: William Hyde Wollaston in 1803

Origin of name: It is named after the asteroid Pallas, which was also discovered in 1803.

Palladium is a soft, silvery metal that is used as a catalyst in the chemical industry and in the catalytic converters in cars, which are used to reduce air pollution. An ideal gasoline engine would emit only water vapor, carbon dioxide, and nitrogen. In real life, however, an engine also emits nitrogen oxides, carbon monoxide, and various unburned hydrocarbons. Because these gases are major contributors to air pollution, car manufacturers have had to find ways to eliminate them. One of these is the catalytic converter. It is a pipe containing a ceramic honeycomb covered with tiny particles of platinum and palladium. As the molecules of the unwanted exhaust gases from the engine pass through the honeycomb, the metal causes them to combine with oxygen to form harmless water vapor and carbon dioxide. None of the metal itself is used up in this process. (A catalyst is any substance that assists or causes a chemical reaction without actually taking part in it.)

The Lore of the Elements

Palladium, which is highly resistant to corrosion, is often alloyed with gold and silver to make dental fixtures harder. Hydrogen will pass through heated palladium, so it is used as a filter for the gas to remove impurities from it. At room temperature, palladium will absorb up to nine hundred times its own volume of hydrogen. While palladium has no known biological function, some palladium compounds may be useful in treating cancer.

Atomic weight: 106.42
Melting point: 2825.6°F (1552°C)

#47 Silver Ag

Discovery: Known since ancient times

Origin of name: It comes from *argentum*, the Latin word for silver, from which it also gets its chemical symbol, Ag.

Silver is a shiny metal that takes a high polish. Because silver is a beautiful, relatively soft metal that is easily worked, it has been used for thousands of years for jewelry, coins, and works of art. Nonsilver objects, such as knives, forks, and spoons, are often plated with a thin coating of the metal. It is also used in making mirrors and in photography, since many silver compounds are very sensitive to light. When exposed to light, substances such as silver bromide turn dark. All of the tones of gray in a black-and-white photograph are actually tiny grains of light-darkened silver compounds. A chemical then "fixes" these tones so that light won't darken the silver any further.

Silver is also used to make dental appliances and in brazing and soldering. Since silver is the best conductor of heat and electricity among all of the elements, it is used in batteries, printed circuitry, and for making electrical contacts, though it is too expensive to use in general household circuitry. Although corrosion-resistant, silver tarnishes easily, because a black sulfide forms on its surface from sulfur compounds in the air that are released as plants decay. Silver has no known biological function.

Atomic weight: 107.87
Melting point: 1763.474°F (961.93°C)

#48 Cadmium Cd

Discovery: Friedrich Stromeyer in 1817

Origin of name: It comes from *cadmia*, the Latin word for the mineral calamine.

Cadmium is a very soft, silvery metal used in the manufacture of nickel-cadmium (or NiCad) batteries, which can be recharged repeatedly. It is also used in making red and yellow pigments for paint. The blue and green colors in the screen of a color television are produced by cadmium **phosphors**, which are tiny specks of material that emit light when struck by electrons. One of its more important functions is in the rods that are used to control nuclear reactors. Since cadmium is an excellent absorber of neutrons, the particles that maintain a nuclear reaction, when rods made of cadmium are inserted or withdrawn from a reactor, the chain reaction inside can be controlled. When neutrons are absorbed by the cadmium, the reaction slows down. When the rods are withdrawn, more neutrons are available, and the reaction speeds up. Cadmium is toxic, and even small amounts can cause serious health problems.

Atomic weight: 112.41
Melting point: 609.62°F (320.9°C)

#49

Indium

In

Discovery: Ferdinand Reich and H. Richter in 1863

Origin of name: It comes from *indigo*, the brightest color in indium's spectrum.

Indium is a rare, soft, silvery-blue metal that is used in making low-melting-point alloys such as those used in overhead sprinkler

Indium ▼

systems. It is also used in making semiconductors and photocells. It can be plated onto glass to make mirrors that are less likely to tarnish than those made with silver. It has no known biological role.

Atomic weight: 114.82
Melting point: 313.898°F (156.61°C)

#50

Tin

Sn

Discovery: Known since ancient times

Origin of name: It is possibly from the Etruscan god Tinia; the symbol, Sn, comes from the Latin *stannum*, a word describing tin's low melting point.

A soft, silvery-white metal, tin is rarely used in its pure state—below 55°F (13°C), it turns into a powder. It is also too soft to be used to make tools or weapons or in construction. Instead, tin is plated onto other metals such as steel to protect them from rusting. "Tin" cans are actually steel cans that have been plated with a thin layer of tin. Alloys of tin were among the first metals to be worked by human beings. Bronze, a mixture of tin and copper, was used by the ancient Egyptians more than five thousand years ago. When alloyed with lead, tin makes **solder**, a low-melting-point metal used to make connections in electrical equipment. Pewter, used in making decorative plates, cups, and other utensils, is an alloy of tin, copper, bismuth, and antimony. Plate glass is manufactured by floating molten glass on a pool of molten tin. Tin is also used in making a special paint that keeps barnacles from attaching to the bottoms of ships. Tin is nontoxic and has no known role in human biology.

Atomic weight: 118.71
Melting point: 449.42°F (231.9°C)

Lead-free ▶
tin fishing weights

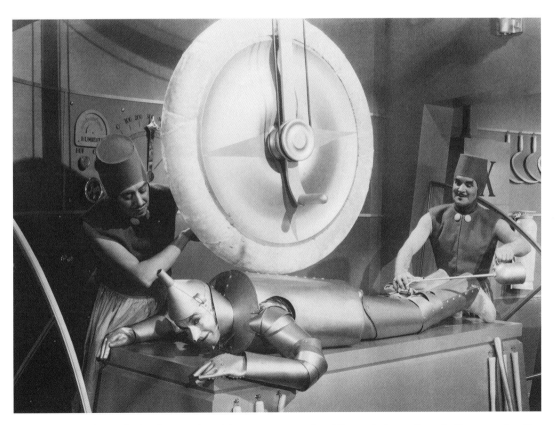

▲ *Because sheet tin is cheap, durable, easy to work with, and doesn't rust, thousands of different products were made with it, from toys to the roofs of houses. One well-known use was for the Tin Man in L. Frank Baum's classic story,* The Wizard of Oz *(1900).*

#51

Antimony
Sb

Discovery: Discovered in the Middle Ages

Origin of name: It comes from the Greek words *anti monos*, meaning "not alone"; its symbol, Sb, comes from the Latin word for stibnite, the ore in which antimony is found.

Antimony is a fairly rare semimetal that is hard, gray, and brittle. The ore in which antimony is found—a black compound called stibnite—was used by women in ancient times as mascara. Today, antimony is used as an alloy to harden other metals, especially lead. It is also used in the manufacture of semiconductors and safety matches. Various compounds of antimony are used in making paints, glass, PVC plastics, and pottery. The metal itself and many of its compounds are poisonous.

Atomic weight: 121.75
Melting point: 1166°F (630°C)

Antimony (seen here in ▶ powdered form)

#52

Tellurium
Te

Discovery: Baron Franz Muller von Reichenstein in 1783

Origin of name: It is named for Earth, which is *Tellus* in Latin.

Tellurium is a rare, brittle, silvery semi-metal. Its cousins on the periodic table include such nonmetals as oxygen and sulfur. It is used in alloys of copper and stainless steel, making them easier to machine, and it improves the strength of lead and its resistance to sulfuric acid. It is also used in the manufacture of semiconductors. Tellurium is one of the rare elements that will combine with gold, and many gold ores are composed of gold tellurides. The mining town of Telluride, Colorado, got its name from the tellurium gold ore found there.

Tellurium not only has no known biological function, but it is very poisonous and can cause birth defects. Even the smallest amounts of tellurium compounds are poisonous. Weirdly enough, contact with even the tiniest amount leads to a long-lasting, garliclike body odor.

Atomic weight: 127.6
Melting point: approximately 841.1°F (449.5°C)

#53

Iodine

Discovery: Bernard Courtois in 1811

Origin of name: It comes from the Greek word *iodes*, meaning "violet," referring to the deep purple-black color of the crystals.

▲ *Seaweed is a good source of dietary iodine.*

Iodine appears in the form of dark violet crystals. At room temperature, these evaporate into a purple gas that has a sharp, distinctive odor. It is highly reactive and combines readily with other elements. It is usually obtained from the mineral sodium iodate as well as from brine (saltwater) pumped from wells. Seaweeds harvested from the oceans also contain large amounts of iodine.

Silver iodide is used in the manufacture of photographic paper. It is also used in "cloud seeding," where crystals of silver iodide are released into clouds by aircraft. Water droplets form around the crystals until they are large enough to fall as rain. The silver iodide is harmless, and eventually dissolves and washes away.

Since the iodine in our bodies concentrates in the thyroid gland, radioactive iodine can be used to trace diseases in the thyroid. After a patient drinks a small amount of radioactive sodium iodide, a doctor can trace the course of the substance and measure the rate at which the thyroid gland absorbs it. This gives doctors valuable information about the health of the gland. Radioactive iodine is also used in the treatment of various types of cancer. Since radioactive iodine has a half-life of only eight days, it does not remain radioactive long enough to do any harm.

Dissolved in alcohol, iodine makes an excellent antiseptic. Iodine salts (iodides) are used in photography, pharmaceuticals, and for making dyes. Although poisonous, in very small amounts iodine is an essential part of our diet, where it helps create the thyroid enzyme, which is important in controlling growth. A deficiency of iodine can lead to diseases of the thyroid gland, so potassium iodide is often added to ordinary table salt, creating iodized salt. You can get all the iodine you need from this, but other sources include seafood and some dairy products.

Atomic weight: 126.9
Melting point: 236.3°F (113.5°C)

#54

Xenon
Xe

Discovery: Sir William Ramsay and M. W. Travers in 1898

Origin of name: It comes from *Xenos*, the Greek word for "strange."

Xenon is a dense, colorless, odorless gas. Aside from research purposes, its main commercial use is in the manufacture of strobe lights for photography because it will emit a bright white light when electricity is passed through it. Almost totally inert, like the other noble gases, xenon will form compounds with fluorine. Scientists have also managed to create some xenon oxides, acids, and salts. Xenon has no role in human biology, and xenon compounds can be very poisonous.

Atomic weight: 131.29
Melting point: −169.42°F (−111.9°C)

◄ *Xenon is used in strobe lights since it produces a bright white light when an electric current passes through it.*

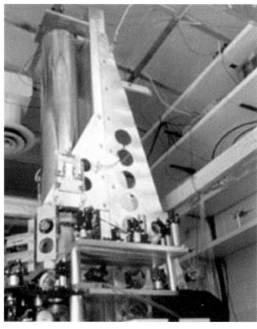

▲ *The cesium clock sets the standard for time in the United States. It is so accurate that it will not gain or lose a single second in twenty million years.*

#55

Cesium
Cs

Discovery: Robert Bunsen and Gustav R. Kirchhoff in 1860

Origin of name: It comes from *caesius*, the Latin word for "sky blue."

Cesium is a soft, silvery metal that reacts actively with oxygen and explosively with water. It will melt if held in the hand. Of the metals, only mercury has a lower melting point. Because cesium is so reactive, it is never found in its natural state. This reactivity has made the metal useful in removing residual gases from vacuums, such as those found inside television tubes. Since tiny amounts of different substances are released when such tubes operate, a small sample of cesium inside the tube will absorb them. Cesium is also used in the making of special types of glass and catalysts. Atomic clocks—accurate to 5 seconds in 300 years—use the resonance frequency of the cesium atom and are the basis for the standard measure of time. Cesium has no known biological function and is nontoxic.

Atomic weight: 132.91
Melting point: 83.3°F (28.5°C)

#56
Barium
Ba

Discovery: Sir Humphry Davy in 1808

Origin of name: It takes its name from *barys*, the Greek word for "heavy."

Barium is a soft, silvery metal similar to lead. Like most of the alkali metals, it oxidizes rapidly, reacts with water, and must be stored in oil or in an inert gas. It is a heavy metal that is easily detected by X-rays, so "barium meals" and "barium enemas" of nontoxic barium sulfate are given to people suffering from disorders of the digestive tract. X-rays can then easily reveal the action of the stomach and intestines to doctors. Other than this, barium has few important commercial uses, although barium nitrate is used to produce green colors in fireworks. Barium has no known biological function and is very toxic in its elemental form.

Atomic weight: 137.33
Melting point: 1337°F (725°C)

THE LANTHANIDES

The lanthanide series of elements are also known as the rare earth elements. ("Rare earth" just means that most of them were discovered in scarce minerals called "rare earths.") The series gets its name from lanthanum, the first element in the group. It consists of the elements from lanthanum (#57) through lutetium (#71). All of the elements in this series are distinguished by having their additional electrons buried inside the atoms instead of being in the outermost orbits. This means that the elements in the lanthanide series are all very much alike since the properties of elements that make them distinctly different from one another are determined by the electrons in the outer orbits.

#57

Lanthanum
La

Discovery: Carl Gustav Mosander in 1839

Origin of name: It comes from a Greek word meaning "hidden."

Lanthanum is a very soft, silvery-white metal that tarnishes and burns easily. It is the first element in the series of elements to which it has given its name: the lanthanides. All of the lanthanides resemble one another very closely.

Lanthanum is used in making special types of optical glass, flints for cigarette lighters, and electrodes for arc lights. Lanthanum has no known biological function, and the element and its compounds are very poisonous.

Atomic weight: 138.91
Melting point: 1688°F (920°C)

▲ *Lanthanum*

Cerium ▶

#58

Cerium
Ce

Discovery: Jöns Jakob Berzelius and W. Hisinger in 1803; isolated for the first time in 1875

Origin of name: It was named after the asteroid Ceres, which was discovered in 1801.

Although cerium, a malleable iron-gray metal, is found abundantly, it is rarely used because it tarnishes readily, reacts with water, and burns when heated. In fact, it may ignite if only just scratched with a metal object. Like lanthanum, it is used in making special types of glass, flints for cigarette lighters, and electrodes for arc lights. It has no known biological role.

Atomic weight: 140.12
Melting point: approximately 1463°F (795°C)

#59

Praseodymium

Pr

Discovery: Baron Carl Auer von Welsbach in 1885; not obtained as a pure metal until 1931

Origin of name: It was named from Greek words meaning "green twin," because of the green color of praseodymium oxide and because it was one of two elements Welsbach found in the mineral didymium.

Praseodymium is a soft, silvery metal. Like many of the other lanthanides, it is used in making hard, corrosion-resistant alloys for aircraft and automobile parts, flints for cigarette lighters, carbon arc lights, and in the special glass used in goggles for welders and glassblowers. Praseodymium salts are also used to create brilliant yellow colors in glass and enamels. It must be stored in oil because it reacts rapidly with oxygen.

Atomic weight: 140.91
Melting point: approximately 1715°F (935°C)

#60

Neodymium

Nd

Discovery: Baron Carl Auer von Welsbach in 1885

Origin of name: Its name comes from Greek words meaning "new twin," since Welsbach discovered two new elements in the same substance he had been studying (the other was praseodymium).

Neodymium is a silvery lanthanide metal employed in making colored glass and ceramic glazes, as well as in alloys for lighter flints and magnets. Magnets made from an alloy of neodymium, iron, and boron are among the most powerful available. The deep red tint neodymium gives to glass is useful for filtering out infrared light. Neodymium is also used in making the artificial rubies used in lasers. It must be stored in oil to prevent it from tarnishing, since it reacts rapidly with oxygen.

Atomic weight: 144.24
Melting point: 1869.53°F (1020.85°C)

A neodymium magnet is ▶ *powerful enough to lift a dollar bill by the iron in the ink.*

#61
Promethium
Pm

Discovery: J. A. Mirinsky in 1945

Origin of name: It was named for the mythical Greek hero Prometheus, who stole the secret of fire from the gods.

Promethium is a radioactive lanthanide element with a half-life of only eighteen years. The element is not found naturally on Earth, although its existence was predicted by the periodic table. It has been detected, however, in the spectrum of some stars. Promethium is created artificially by bombarding neodymium and praseodymium with neutrons, **deuterons**, and alpha particles. Since it can convert light directly into electricity, promethium is used commercially in the manufacture of solar batteries.

Atomic weight: 145
Melting point: 1907.33°F (1041.85°C)

#62
Samarium
Sm

Discovery: Paul-Émile Lecoq de Boisbaudran in 1879

Origin of name: It was named for the mineral samarskite, in which it was discovered.

Samarium is a rare, silvery lanthanide metal used in making special types of lasers, ceramics, magnets, and infrared-absorbing glass. It will ignite spontaneously at temperatures above 302°F (150°C). It is nontoxic and has no known role in biology.

Atomic weight: 150.36
Melting point: 1964.93°F (1073.85°C)

Samarium ▼

The Lore of the Elements

▲ Europium

Discovery: Jean-Claude Galissard de Maringnac and Paul-Émile Lecoq de Boisbaudran in 1880

Origin of name: It was named after the Finnish chemist Johan Gadolin.

Gadolinium is a malleable, silvery lanthanide metal used, as are many of its related elements, in making alloys for magnets and electronics. Very small amounts added to iron and chromium alloys increase their resistance to high temperatures and oxidation. Like several other rare earth elements, gadolinium is used in making the color phosphors that coat the inside of color television tubes.

Atomic weight: 157.25
Melting point: 2393.33°F (1311.85°C)

#63

Europium
Eu

Discovery: Eugéne-Anatole Demarçay in 1901

Origin of name: It was named after the continent of Europe.

Europium, the rarest of the lanthanide elements, is a soft, silvery metal used in making alloys for superconductors and lasers, as well as in the manufacture of the fluorescent light tubes and red phosphors in color television tubes. It is also used in control rods for nuclear reactors since it absorbs more neutrons than any other element. Like samarium, it will ignite spontaneously at temperatures above 302°F (150°C). It must be stored in oil since it reacts rapidly with water and air.

Atomic weight: 151.97
Melting point: 1511.6°F (822.0°C)

▲ Gadolinium

#65

Terbium

Tb

Discovery: Carl Gustaf Mosander in 1843

Origin of name: It was named, like the elements Yttrium, Erbium, and Ytterbium, after the Swedish town of Ytterby, where the element was mined.

Terbium is a silver-gray lanthanide metal soft enough to be cut with a knife. It resembles lead, but is much heavier. It is used in making lasers and other electronic devices, as well as in the green phosphors in color television tubes.

Atomic weight: 158.92
Melting point: 2472.53°F (1355.85°C)

▲ *Dysprosium*

#66

Dysprosium

Dy

Discovery: Paul-Émile Lecoq de Boisbaudran in 1886

Origin of name: It comes from *dysprositos*, a Greek word meaning "hard to get" because of the difficulty involved in its detection and isolation.

Dysprosium is a silvery metal that, like many of the other lanthanide metals, is soft enough to be cut with a knife. It is used in the manufacture of color television tubes and in alloys used in making magnets. It is also used in making nuclear reactor control rods, since it absorbs neutrons well. It reacts rapidly with water and air.

Atomic weight: 162.50
Melting point: 2573.33°F (1411.85°C)

▲ *Terbium*

#67

Holmium

Ho

Discovery: Per Teodor Cleve in 1878

Origin of name: It comes from Holmia, the Latin name for the city of Stockholm.

Holmium is a rare, soft, silvery metal used, as many of the other lanthanides, in coloring glass and in the manufacture of magnets. It is also used in making nuclear reactor control rods, since it absorbs neutrons well.

Atomic weight: 164.93
Melting point: 2684.93°F (1473.85°C)

▲ *Holmium*

#68

Erbium

Er

Discovery: Carl Gustaf Mosander in 1842

Origin of name: It was named, like Yttrium, Ytterbium, and Terbium, after the Swedish town of Ytterby, where the element was mined.

Erbium is a rare soft, silver-gray lanthanide metal used in making alloys and infrared-absorbing glass used in safety goggles for welders.

Atomic weight: 167.26
Melting point: 2783.93°F (1528.85°C)

#69

Thulium

Tm

Discovery: Per Teodor Cleve in 1879

Origin of name: It was named for Thule, the ancient name for Scandinavia.

Thulium is a silvery metal that, like most of the lanthanide metals, is soft enough to cut with a knife. Although rare and therefore too expensive for wide commercial use, thulium has been used in making lasers and portable X-ray machines.

Atomic weight: 168.93
Melting point: 2812.73°F (1544.85°C)

#70

Ytterbium
Yb

Discovery: Jean-Charles Galissard de Marignac in 1878

Origin of name: It was named, like the elements Yttrium, Erbium, and Terbium, after the Swedish town of Ytterby, where the element was mined.

Ytterbium, a soft, silvery metal, was the first of the lanthanide elements to be discovered. Although it is more abundant in Earth's crust than tin, it is rarely used outside of research purposes. Its limited commercial use has been in making stronger alloys of stainless steel.

Atomic weight: 173.04
Melting point: 1505.93°F (818.85°C)

Ytterbium ▶

#71

Lutetium
Lu

Discovery: Independently discovered by Georges Urbain and Carl Auer von Welsbach in 1907

Origin of name: It comes from Lutetia, the Latin name for Paris.

The discovery of lutetium was as complicated as the plot of a soap opera. It began when Carl Gustav Mosander found two new elements—erbia and terbia—in a sample of yttrium. In 1860 the Swedish chemist Nils Johan Berlin suggested that Mosander's erbia was not an element after all. He transferred the name erbia to what had been called terbia. In 1878, Marignac showed that Berlin's terbia was composed of two rare earths: terbia itself and ytterbia. In 1879, L. F. Nilson divided ytterbia into ytterbia and scandia. In 1907, Nilson's ytterbia was separated by French chemist Georges Urbain into neoytterbia and lutecia. Carl Auer von Welsbach, who had isolated them himself at about the same time, proposed the names Aldebaranium and Cassiopeium for the new elements, though these were not officially adopted. Urbain's suggestion of lutecia was later changed to lutetium.

The hardest, densest and one of the rarest of the lanthanide elements (for one

The Lore of the Elements

reason because it is extremely difficult to extract from the minerals in which it it found), lutetium is a silvery metal that has virtually no use outside of scientific research.

Atomic weight: 174.97
Melting point: 3025°F (1663°C)

#72

Hafnium

Hf

Discovery: Dirk Coster and George Karl von Hevesy in 1923

Origin of name: It derives its name from Hafnia, the Latin name for Copenhagen.

Hafnium is a silvery, corrosion-resistant metal that is chemically very similar to the element zirconium. In the presence of oxygen, it produces a thin film that prevents further oxidation, much in the same way that aluminum does. An excellent absorber of neutrons, hafnium is used primarily in the manufacture of control rods for nuclear reactors.

Atomic weight: 178.49
Melting point: approximately 4047.53°F (2230.85°C)

#73

Tantalum

Ta

Discovery: Anders Gustav Ekeberg in 1802

Origin of name: It derives its name from the Greek mythological character Tantalus, the father of Niobe, the queen of the city of Thebes.

Originally believed to be identical to niobium, tantalum is a hard, dense, silver-gray metal. Very resistant to corrosion, it also causes no immune reactions in humans. For this reason, it is used to make surgical appliances that need to be embedded permanently in the human body, such as replacement hip joints and special foils and wires for repairing torn nerves. As an alloy, tantalum adds corrosion-resistance to other metals, as well as hardness and a higher melting point. For these reasons, tantalum alloys are useful in the manufacture of parts for jets, rockets, and other devices that produce high temperatures. Tantalum is also used widely in making electronic parts and a substance called tantalum oxide, which is one of the hardest materials ever created.

Atomic weight: 180.95
Melting point: approximately 5467.73°F (3019.85°C)

▼ *Tantalum*

#74

Tungsten

W

Discovery: Fausto and Juan José de Elhuar in 1783

Origin of name: The name comes from the Swedish words for "heavy stone," and its chemical symbol, W, comes from the German word *wolfram*, which is derived from the words for "wolf dirt."

Tungsten had been known as a metal for a long time before it was discovered to be an element. Hard, brittle, and gray, tungsten has the highest melting point of any metal, giving it many industrial uses where strength, hardness, and resistance to high temperatures is important. It is used to make the filaments in lightbulbs, which is one of its most important applications. Tungsten carbide is extremely hard and is widely used in manufacturing high-speed cutting tools of all kinds.

Atomic weight: 183.85
Melting point: approximately 6191.33°F (3421.85°C)

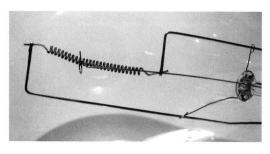

#75

Rhenium

Re

Discovery: Walter Noddack, Ida Eva Tacke-Noddack, and Otto Carl Berg in 1925

Origin of name: It comes from Rhenus, the Greek name for the Rhine River.

One of the rarest of the elements, rhenium is an extremely dense, silvery metal with a melting point second only to tungsten. It is used in electric light filaments and in tungsten and molybdenum alloys, where it adds hardness and resistance to wear. In combination with tungsten, rhenium is used in making thermocouples, or heat-measuring devices, capable of measuring temperatures as high as 3632°F (2000°C). In 1925, 1 million pounds (454,000 kilograms) of ore had to be worked in order to obtain a single gram of rhenium. By the end of the twentieth century, however, improved refining techniques increased the yield to about 1,000 pounds (454 kilograms) a year.

Atomic weight: 186.2
Melting point: 5759.33°F (3181.85°C)

◀ *This is a tungsten filament inside a lightbulb.*

The Lore of the Elements

#76
Osmium
Os

Discovery: Smithson Tennant in 1803

Origin of name: It gets its name from *osme*, the Greek word for "smell."

A rare, silvery metal that is very hard and has good corrosion resistance, osmium is twice as dense as lead, making it the densest of all the elements. A sample the size of a brick weighs nearly 56 pounds (25 kilograms). It got its name from the smelly odor it gives off as it oxidizes. This oxide is very poisonous. Osmium is used in the making of very hard alloys—in which the osmium is harmless—for pen points, needles, electrical contacts, and other applications where hardness and resistance to wear are important. Osmium has no known biological role and is very poisonous.

Atomic weight: 190.2
Melting point: 5513°F (3045°C)

◀ **An osmium-plated pen point**

#77
Iridium
Ir

Discovery: Smithson Tennant in 1803

Origin of name: It comes from the Latin word *iris*, which means "rainbow," because the element's salts are brightly colored.

Iridium is a very rare, hard, silvery-yellow metal. The most corrosion-resistant element known, it is used in making very hard, resilient platinum and osmium alloys for electrical contacts and rocket engines. An alloy of platinum and iridium was used to make the standard meter bar, kept in Paris, France, on which all metric measurements are based.

Although iridium is rare on Earth, it is a fairly common element in many meteorites and asteroids. When scientists found a layer of iridium in Earth's surface, it was the first clue to the discovery that a giant asteroid impacted our planet 65 million years ago. Hitting Earth near the Yucatán Peninsula of Mexico, it may have caused the demise of the dinosaurs by radically altering the climate of Earth.

Atomic weight: 192.2
Melting point: approximately 4436.33°F (2446.85°C)

#78

Platinum
Pt

Discovery: Known and used by pre-Columbian American Indians. It was found by Englishman Charles Wood in 1741 and first taken to Europe in 1750.

Origin of name: It comes from *platina*, the Spanish word for "silver."

Platinum is a rare, silvery metal. It is considered, along with gold and silver, to be one of the precious metals (only 80 tons are mined every year). It is very corrosion-resistant and does not react with oxygen. As a precious metal, it is used in making jewelry. It is used in dentistry and in making medical equipment and implants, such as pacemakers. It is also used in the manufacture of the catalytic converters that remove pollutants from the exhaust of automobiles.

▲ *Platinum is a vital part of the catalytic converter used in cars to reduce air pollution.*

Just as a bar of platinum-iridium alloy is the standard meter, another bar of the same alloy forms the basis for the standard kilogram, the basic unit of mass in the metric system. Platinum has no known biological function, but recent research suggests that it may inhibit the growth of certain types of cancer.

Atomic weight: 195.08
Melting point: 3216.11°F (1768.95°C)

#79

Gold
Au

Discovery: Known since ancient times

Origin of name: *Gold* is the Anglo-Saxon word for the metal; the symbol is derived from *aurum*, the Latin word for "gold."

Gold is a soft, yellow metal that is extremely resistant to corrosion. It occurs in its natural state but is also mined, mostly in South Africa and Russia, where about 1,650 tons (1,500 metric tons) are obtained every year. Most of this is stored in the form of bullion, or gold bars. Its bright yellow color and resistance to tarnishing caused it to be used for thousands of years in making jewelry and coins. Since gold is also soft and malleable, it can be beaten into extremely thin sheets called gold leaf. One ounce

Gold jewelry

(28.3 grams) of gold can be beaten into a sheet covering 300 square feet (28 square meters), which might be only four to five millionths of an inch in thickness. This can be applied to all sorts of objects, from statuary to the roofs of Cambodian temples, in a process known as **gilding**.

Gold is one of the most inert of all the metals and rarely combines with any other elements. Even nitric acid will not touch it. For this reason, it is very useful in applications where extreme resistance to corrosion is important. Dentists use gold to make replacements for teeth that last for an entire lifetime. Since gold is an excellent conductor of electricity and is resistant to corrosion, it has wide use in electronics. A good reflector of infrared radiation, gold leaf is used to protect spacecraft instruments from heat. A thin coating of gold—so thin it can be seen through—is used on the face plates of astronauts' helmets to filter dangerous rays from the sun. Gold has no known biological function, though it is used in some treatments for arthritis.

Atomic weight: 196.97
Melting point: 1947.97°F (1064.43°C)

#80
Mercury
Hg

Discovery: Known since ancient times

Origin of name: Named for the planet Mercury. The symbol is derived from the Latin word *hydragyrum*, meaning "liquid silver." Another name for mercury is quicksilver, which means "living silver."

Mercury is the only metal that is liquid at room temperature. It is bright silver in color and very heavy. It is obtained from a bright red ore called cinnabar. Most mercury comes from Spain, where it has been mined for more than two thousand years. Mercury freezes at −37.9°F (−38.8°C) and boils at 674.11°F (356.73°C). This wide range of temperatures makes it useful in scientific instruments such as thermometers. Its weight makes it useful in barometers, which is why atmospheric pressure is measured in "inches of mercury." Good use is made of its excellent electrical conductivity in thermostats and silent wall switches. Energy-efficient mercury vapor lamps—recognizable by their bluish light—are used to illuminate parking lots and other large areas.

Mercury readily absorbs other elements, forming substances called **amalgams**. For instance, the silver filling dentists use to repair a cavity is actually an amalgam of powdered silver and mercury.

Compounds of mercury were once used in making pharmaceuticals (though very rarely anymore, now that mercury's toxic nature is well known) and are still used in making pesticides. The presence of mercury in rivers, lakes, and oceans has been recognized as a major pollutant. Among other things, it can contaminate seafood, which is then eaten by humans. For this reason the use of many substances containing the element has been banned.

Mercury is extremely toxic and is easily absorbed and stored by the body. You can absorb the element directly through the skin and even its vapors are poisonous. In the 1800s, mercury was widely employed in treating the felt and beaver fur used in making hats. The hatters doing this absorbed mercury into their bodies, where it attacked their nervous systems. Since the cause of the strange behavior this resulted in was unknown, everyone assumed that many hatters were simply mad. So common was this idea that the Mad Hatter became a character in *Alice in Wonderland*.

Atomic weight: 200.59
Melting point: −37.9°F (−38.8°C)

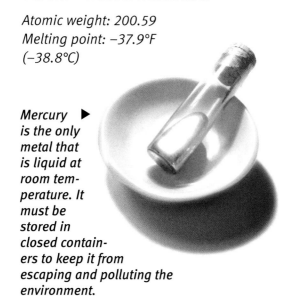

Mercury ▶ *is the only metal that is liquid at room temperature. It must be stored in closed containers to keep it from escaping and polluting the environment.*

Thallium ▶

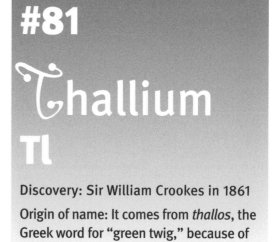

#81
Thallium
Tl

Discovery: Sir William Crookes in 1861

Origin of name: It comes from *thallos*, the Greek word for "green twig," because of the bright green line of its spectrum.

Thallium is a very soft, gray metal similar to lead, although unlike lead, it tarnishes readily when exposed to air. Since thallium and its compounds are highly toxic—it was once used as a rat poison, but that application is now generally banned—its uses are limited, other than in the manufacture of glass with a high index of refraction (the ability to bend light). Contact with thallium may be both carcinogenic and the cause of birth defects.

Atomic weight: 204.38
Melting point: 579°F (305.85°C)

#82

Lead
Pb

Discovery: Known since ancient times

Origin of name: The word *lead* is Anglo-Saxon, while the symbol, Pb, comes from the Latin word for lead, *plumbum*. This is the same word that *plumber* comes from, since plumbers once worked with lead pipes, which were called plumbing.

Lead is a soft, dark gray metal that is easily worked. Because of its heavy weight and low melting point, lead has been used for centuries in making bullets. In the past, many soldiers and hunters were able to cast their own bullets. In modern times, however, lead shot has been banned for use in hunting since so much was being used that it was becoming a pollution hazard. Lead was also once widely used in typesetting, where all of the letters on the page of a book, magazine, or newspaper were printed from individual lead "slugs." The word *leading* is still used to describe the space between lines of type, even when the type has been set by a computer.

Lead was once widely used for making all sorts of things, from coins to appliances, as well as in the production of pewter and paint. White lead was once one of the most popular paints used in homes. Most domestic uses for lead, however, have been banned since it can be very dangerous to human health. Lead also was once added to gasoline to make it burn more smoothly, but this use has been banned as well, since it was a major source of dangerous pollutants.

Lead is still used in the manufacture of car batteries, glass, ammunition, and radiation shielding. Lead crystal glass is prized for its clarity and brilliance. One of lead's most important uses is as one of the components of solder, a low-melting-point alloy used in making connections in electrical devices.

Atomic weight: 207
Melting point: 621.5°F (327.5°C)

▼ *Before the dangers of lead were well known, toys such as this rocket were made of lead.*

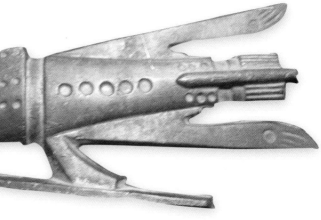

#83

Bismuth
Bi

Discovery: Known since the fifteenth century

Origin of name: Bismuth comes from the Latin word *bisemutum*, which in turn comes from the German *weisse masse*, which means "white mass."

Bismuth is a brittle, dense, pinkish-silver metal. It shares with water the rare quality of expanding when changing from liquid form to solid. For this reason, it is used in making alloys that remain at a constant volume when they solidify, which is useful in the manufacture of molds. Bismuth is also used in making the low-melting-point alloys used in solder, fuses, and fire detectors. In a fuse, for instance, the heat caused by a sudden surge of electrical current will cause the bismuth alloy to melt and break the circuit. Bismuth is also used in making yellow pigments and in some medications. Bismuth carbonate, for instance, is taken to ease indigestion.

Atomic weight: 208.98
Melting point: 520.6°F (271.4°C)

Bismuth ▶
crystal

#84

Polonium
Po

Discovery: Marie Curie in 1888

Origin of name: Curie named it after her native Poland.

Polonium, the first element to be discovered by Marie Curie in her search to discover the source of uranium's radioactivity, is an extremely rare, silvery, radioactive metal that is used as a heat source in unmanned spacecraft and in tiny amounts in devices that produce alpha particles for scientific research. Since polonium is highly radioactive, some five thousand times more so than radium, it is a very dangerous substance. The isotope polonium-210 is 100 billion times more toxic than cyanide.

Atomic weight: 209
Melting point: 488.93°F (253.85°C)

#85

Astatine

At

Discovery: Dale R. Corson in 1940

Origin of name: It comes from *astatos*, the Greek word for "unstable."

Astatine is a highly radioactive element that was created by bombarding bismuth with alpha particles. Less than 1 millionth of a gram has ever been produced. No one knows much about the physical characteristics or possible uses for astatine. Since it has a half-life of only 8.3 hours it simply is not around long enough to study. Astatine occurs naturally in Earth's crust as a product of the decay of uranium and thorium, but it is estimated that at any one time there is less than 1 ounce (28 grams) on the planet.

Atomic weight: 210
Melting point: 638.33°F (336.85°C)

#86

Radon

Rn

Discovery: Friedrich Ernst Dorn in 1900

Origin of name: Radon's name is derived from *radium*.

Radon is the densest of all the gaseous elements. It is produced during the decay of radium. While it is colorless, odorless, and chemically inert, it is nevertheless extremely dangerous because of its radioactivity. One of its early uses was in the treatment of cancer, though it is no longer used for this. Radon is produced naturally in Earth's crust as radioactive elements decay. In certain parts of the country, radon can collect in cellars and basements. Since too much radon can be a health hazard, many homeowners install radon gas detectors.

Atomic weight: 222
Melting point: −96°F (−71°C)

#88

Radium
Ra

Discovery: Marie and Pierre Curie in 1898

Origin of name: It is taken from the Latin word *radius*, meaning "ray."

#87

Francium
Fr

Discovery: Marguerite Perey in 1939

Origin of name: It is named for France, Perey's homeland.

Francium is a very heavy, extremely radioactive metal with a half-life of only twenty-one minutes. It is a product of the decay of uranium and thorium and, mostly due to its short half-life, has never actually been seen. It is thought that there is less than 1 ounce (28 grams) of francium in Earth's crust at any given time.

Atomic weight: 223
Melting point: 80.33°F (26.85°C)

Radium is a silvery-white radioactive metal found naturally in uranium ores. However, it is an extremely rare element since there is only about 0.035 ounce (1 gram) in 6.8 tons (7 metric tons) of ore. After the Curies discovered the presence of radium in uranium ore, it took them four years to actually produce a sample of the metal.

Once called the "wonder metal" because it glowed in the dark and gave off heat, it was used for many years in cancer treatment and for the luminous paint applied to clock and watch dials. This was, however, long before the real dangers of radiation were fully known. Radium is rarely if ever used anymore in medicine and never in paint, since it is so very dangerous to handle. World production is now as little as 3.5 ounces (100 grams) per year.

Radium is heavier than lead and chemically similar to strontium and barium. It is a product of the radioactive decay of thorium-230, which is in turn the product of the decay of uranium-238. Radium itself will eventually decay to form the stable radium G, also known as uranium lead. One of the disintegration products of radium is the gas radon.

Atomic weight: 226
Melting point: 1760°F (960°C)

THE ACTINIDES

The elements from actinium (#89) through lawrencium (#103) are known as the actinide series. Like the lanthanides, the actinides contain their additional electrons deep within the atom instead of in the outer orbits. Since it is the electrons in the outer orbits that determine the unique characteristics of each element, the elements in the actinide series closely resemble each other.

#89

Actinium
Ac

Discovery: André Debierne in 1899

Origin of name: It comes from the Greek word *aktinos*, meaning "ray."

Actinium is a soft, silvery radioactive metal extracted from uranium ores and produced in nuclear reactors. It is so radioactive that it causes the air around it to glow. Only very tiny amounts are produced every year. It has few commercial applications and is used mainly in scientific research.

Atomic weight: 227
Melting point: 1923.53°F (1050.85°C)

#90

Thorium
Th

Discovery: Jöns Jakob Berzelius in 1828

Origin of name: Thorium was named after Thor, the Norse god of war.

Thorium is a soft, silvery metal with one of the highest melting points of all the elements. It is found abundantly on Earth's surface. Its main use has been in the production of gas mantles, the little bags of cloth that fit over the jet in a gas light, such as those in gasoline lanterns. When heated by the burning gas, the thorium in the cloth glows with an intense white light. Thorium is also used as an alloy with magnesium, where it helps make the metal resistant to high temperatures. Thorium's radioactivity was not discovered until 1897, by Henri Becquerel and the Curies. Natural thorium, with a half-life of 14 billion years, is only very weakly radioactive, however.

Atomic weight: 232
Melting point: 3182°F (1750°C)

#91

Protactinium
Pa

Discovery: The isotope Pa-234 was identified by Kasimir Fajans and Otto H. Göhring in 1913. In 1917, two research teams, one led by Otto Hahn and Lise Meitner and the other by Frederick Soddy and John A. Cranston, simultaneously isolated isotope Pa-231, a more stable form of the element.

Origin of name: From the Greek words for first ray. The element was originally named *brevium* (from "brief") because of its short half-life. It did not get its present name until 1949, when it was called protoactinium because it decays into actinium. This was later shortened to protactinium.

Protactinium is a silvery radioactive metal that is the third rarest of the natural elements. Its existence had been predicted by Mendeleyev, who found a space for it in his table. In 1918 a more stable form of the element was discovered almost simultaneously by two different teams of scientists, Otto Hahn and Lise Meitner, and Frederick Soddy and John A. Cranston. Protactinium is found in uranium ores, and only a few hundred grams are known to exist. This is used exclusively in scientific research. Protactinium has no known practical use. It is extremely toxic.

Atomic weight: 231
Melting point: approximately 2861.33°F (1571.85°C)

#92

Uranium
U

Discovery: Martin H. Klaproth in 1789

Origin of name: It is named for the planet Uranus, which had just been discovered.

Uranium is a heavy, silvery-white metal that is the primary source for the fuel for nuclear reactors. Uranium's radioactivity was not discovered until 1896, nearly a century after the element was first found. It was the first radioactive element known. In the 1950s, when the U.S. government was using enormous amounts of the element in the production of atomic energy plants and nuclear bombs, there was a kind of "uranium rush" similar to the gold rush of the 1840s. Thousands of people headed west with Geiger counters (devices for detecting radioactivity) in their hands, and many of them became very rich.

Uranium itself is not very radioactive—the most common isotope, uranium-238,

THE TRANSURANIUM ELEMENTS

Transuranium means "beyond uranium" and describes the elements in the periodic table that fall after uranium. All of these elements have been artificially created in the laboratory and, for the most part, do not exist in nature. Most of them are made by bombarding other elements with neutrons. This process creates a new, even heavier element. For instance, when uranium is bombarded with neutrons, the new artificial element neptunium is created. All of the **transuranium elements** are very radioactive. Atoms heavier than fermium are created by fusing the nuclei of two atoms. For example, elements 101 through 106 (mendelevium through seaborgium) were created by fusing the nuclei of an atom that is slightly lighter than the one that is to be created, such as californium, bismuth, or lead, with the nuclei of light atoms, such as carbon, krypton, or calcium.

Normally, only a very few atoms of these new elements are created at one time. Because of these small quantities and the fact that their half-lives are so short—often only a few milliseconds—these elements are very hard to identify and little is known of their chemical properties.

has a half-life of 4.6 billion years—but many of the elements it decays into are very radioactive. The end product of uranium's decay is lead.

In the late 1930s, German scientists Lisa Meitner and Otto Hahn discovered that the nucleus of the uranium-235 atom could be split in two by the impact of a neutron. When this happened, energy was released along with more neutrons. These new neutrons would then go on to split more uranium atoms. These would release even more energy and even more neutrons—and so on until all the available uranium was used up. Since the process involved the breaking up—or fissioning—of the nucleus of the uranium atom, they called it **nuclear fission**. Meitner and Hahn were able to observe this happening only in very small samples.

In 1944 the Italian-American scientist Enrico Fermi succeeded in initiating con-

trolled nuclear fission on a fairly large scale. Once the process of fission begins, there is no way to stop it, but it can be controlled by limiting the number of neutrons that are available. The fewer neutrons there are, the fewer uranium nuclei will be split. The heat released during nuclear fission is used to make steam, which in turn runs turbine-powered generators to produce electricity.

One of the by-products of the use of uranium-238 in fission reactors is the creation of plutonium-239, which can be fissioned just like uranium. It is plutonium that is used in nuclear weapons. Although uranium is only mildly radioactive, like most heavy metals it is still very poisonous.

Atomic weight: 238
Melting point: approximately 2236.73°F (1224.85°C)

#93

Neptunium
Np

Discovery: Edwin M. McMillan and Philip H. Abelson in 1940

Origin of name: It is named for the planet Neptune.

Neptunium is an artificially created metallic element produced from uranium as a by-product of nuclear reactors. It has few practical uses and is extremely poisonous due to its radioactivity.

Atomic weight: 237
Melting point: approximately 1181.93°F (638.85°C)

#94

Plutonium
Pu

Discovery: Glenn Seaborg, A. C. Wahl, and J. W. Kennedy in 1940

Origin of name: It is named for the planet Pluto.

Plutonium is a silvery-yellow metal that is created artificially from spent uranium nuclear reactor fuel rods. Because it fissions very easily, it can be used as a nuclear fuel itself as well as in nuclear weapons. A single kilogram can produce an explosion equal to about 11,000 tons (10,000 metric tons) of a conventional chemical explosive. It is created in huge quantities in nuclear reactors, and there are special reactors dedicated solely to its production.

An isotope of plutonium, plutonium-238, does not fission. Its radioactivity, however, produces a good deal of heat, which can be transformed into electricity. Since even very small amounts can produce considerable power, it has been used as a source of electrical power on spacecraft.

▲ *Plutonium was the basis for the atomic bomb.*

Plutonium is so radioactive that it would feel warm if you were to touch it. In addition to its radioactivity, plutonium is a fire hazard. It reacts rapidly with oxygen and water. This results in an accumulation of plutonium hydride, a compound that will burn in air at room temperature. When plutonium burns it also greatly expands in size and may burst its container, causing the spread of the radioactive material.

Atomic weight: 244
Melting point: 1183.73°F (639.85)

#95
Americium
Am

Discovery: Glenn Seaborg, Ralph A. James, L. O. Morgan, and Albert Ghiorso in 1944

Origin of name: It is named after the United States of America.

Americium is a rare, artificially created, silvery metal. It is created by bombarding plutonium with neutrons. It is used in extremely small amounts in the production of smoke alarms. An extremely tiny (and safe) quantity of the element in the alarm will ionize the air around it—that is, it removes some of the electrons from the atoms. Ionized air is a good conductor of electricity. As long as the air conducts electricity, the alarm knows that everything is all right. The presence of even a small amount of smoke, however, will de-ionize the air. This breaks the electrical circuit and sets off the alarm. Americium is radioactive and poisonous.

Atomic weight: 243
Melting point: approximately 1821.2°F (994°C)

#96
Curium
Cm

Discovery: Glenn Seaborg, Ralph A. James, and Albert Ghiorso in 1944

Origin of name: It is named for Marie and Pierre Curie.

Curium is an artificially created radioactive metal that is produced from plutonium in nuclear reactors. Since curium's radiation produces heat, which can then be converted into electricity, it is used to generate electrical energy in spacecraft, pacemakers, and remote instruments.

Atomic weight: 247
Melting point: approximately 2456.33°F (1346.85°C)

#97
Berkelium
Bk

Discovery: Stanley G. Thompson, Glenn Seaborg, and Albert Ghiorso in 1949

Origin of name: It is named for Berkeley, California, where it was discovered.

Berkelium is a silvery, radioactive metal produced from plutonium in nuclear reactors. Because it is so extremely rare, it has no known uses.

Atomic weight: 247
Melting point: unknown

#98
Californium
Cf

Discovery: Stanley G. Thompson, Kenneth Street, Albert Ghiorso, and Glenn Seaborg in 1950

Origin of name: It is named for the state of California.

Californium is a rare, radioactive, silvery metal created artificially in nuclear reactors.

Like berkelium, it is too rare to have any known practical use other than in research. It is extremely radioactive and therefore dangerous to handle.

Atomic weight: 251
Melting point: uncertain

#99
Einsteinium
Es

Discovery: Albert Ghiorso in 1952

Origin of name: It is named for Albert Einstein.

Einsteinium was discovered when scientists examined tons of radioactive coral blasted by a nuclear bomb test at Eniwetok Atoll in

◀ *Einsteinium was named in honor of the great physicist Albert Einstein (1879–1955).*

the Pacific Ocean. The sample that was extracted from the coral weighed only one hundred millionth of a gram. A rare radioactive metal created only in tiny amounts in nuclear reactors, its only use is in scientific research.

Atomic weight: 252
Melting point: uncertain

#100

Fermium

Fm

Discovery: Albert Ghiorso in 1952

Origin of name: It is named for Enrico Fermi, the Italian-American scientist who built the first nuclear reactor in 1944.

Like einsteinium, fermium was discovered while examining tons of radioactive coral blasted by a nuclear bomb test at Eniwetok Atoll in the Pacific Ocean. Today it is produced artificially in nuclear reactors, but it has such a short half-life—only twenty hours—that scientists doubt that enough will ever be accumulated to be weighed or even seen. Consequently, it has neither commercial nor research applications.

Atomic weight: 257
Melting point: uncertain

#101

Mendelevium

Md

Discovery: Albert Ghiorso in 1955

Origin of name: It is named for Dimitri Mendeleyev, who developed the periodic table.

Mendelevium is created by bombarding einsteinium with alpha particles. It is so rare—it has a half-life of only fifty-six days—that only a few atoms have ever been formed. It has no known use.

Atomic weight: 258
Melting point: uncertain

#102

ꓠobelium
No

Discovery: Albert Ghiorso in 1958

Origin of name: It is named for Alfred Nobel, inventor of dynamite and founder of the Nobel Prize.

Only a few atoms of nobelium have ever been created, which is done by bombarding curium with the nuclei of carbon atoms. Its rarity combined with a half-life of only fifty-eight minutes means that very little is known about the properties of nobelium. Discovery of the element had originally been claimed by scientists at the Nobel Institute in Stockholm, Sweden, but this was shown to be a false identification. When Albert Ghiorso and his team discovered the element, they retained the name originally suggested by the Swedish scientists. Because of its extreme rarity, it has not even been possible to study nobelium, let alone find a use for it.

Atomic weight: 259
Melting point: uncertain

#103

ꓡawrencium
Lr

Discovery: Albert Ghiorso in 1961

Origin of name: It is named for the physicist Ernest Lawrence, the inventor of the cyclotron.

Only a few atoms of lawrencium have ever been created, by bombarding californium with the nuclei of boron atoms. Because of its rarity, and a half-life of only three minutes, little is known about its properties.

Atomic weight: 260
Melting point: uncertain

◀ *Nobelium was named in honor of Alfred Nobel (1833–1896), the inventor of dynamite and founder of the Nobel Prize.*

#104

Rutherford-ium

Rf

Discovery: Independently by a team of scientists working in Russia, and Albert Ghiorso working in the United States, in 1969

Origin of name: It is named for Sir Ernest Rutherford.

Only a few atoms of rutherfordium have ever been created, by bombarding californium with the nuclei of carbon atoms. Because of rutherfordium's rarity and its half-life of between only 0.013 second and 62 seconds (depending on the isotope), very little is known about its properties.

Atomic weight: 261
Melting point: unknown

#105

Dubnium

Db

Discovery: Found in 1970, the priority for the discovery of this element is disputed

Origin of name: It is named for the Russian town of Dubna, a major center of scientific research.

Only a few atoms of dubnium have ever been created. This is done by bombarding californium with nitrogen nuclei. Because of its rarity and its half-life of only 34 seconds—and as short as 1.2 seconds, depending on the isotope—very little is known about dubnium's properties.

Atomic weight: 262
Melting point: unknown

#106

Seaborgium
Sg

Discovery: Albert Ghiorso in 1974

Origin of name: It is named for Glenn Seaborg, winner of the 1951 Nobel Prize for the discovery of plutonium.

#107

Bohrium
Bh

Discovery: P. Armbruster and G. Münzenberg in 1981

Origin of name: It is named for Danish physicist Niels Bohr.

Only a few atoms of seaborgium have ever been created. This is done by bombarding californium with oxygen nuclei. Between seaborgium's rarity and a half-life of between 2.8 and 4×10^{-3} seconds (depending on the isotope), little is known about its chemical properties other than that they seem to resemble those of tungsten. The only research that has been done on the element used a sample consisting of only seven atoms!

Atomic weight: 263
Melting point: unknown

Only a few atoms of bohrium have ever been created. This is done by bombarding bismuth with chromium atoms. Between its rarity and a half-life of between 0.1 and 8×10^{-3} seconds (depending on the isotope), little is known about the properties of bohrium.

Atomic weight: 262
Melting point: unknown

◀ *Physicist Glenn Seaborg (1913–1999) points to seaborgium, the element named in his honor.*

#108

Hassium

Hs

Discovery: P. Armbruster and G. Münzenberg in 1984

Origin of name: It is named after the German state of Hesse.

Only a few atoms of hassium have ever been created. This is done by bombarding lead with iron atoms. Between hassium's rarity and a half-life of between 8×10^{-5} and 2×10^{-3} seconds (depending on the isotope), little is known about its properties.

Atomic weight: 265
Melting point: unknown

#109

Meitnerium

Mt

Discovery: Peter Armbruster and Gottfried Münzenberg in 1982

Origin of name: It is named for physicist Lise Meitner, who first proposed the possibility of splitting the uranium nucleus.

Fewer than ten atoms of meitnerium have ever been created. This is done by bombarding bismuth with iron atoms. Between its extreme rarity and a half-life of approximately 3.4×10^{-3} seconds, little is known about meitnerium's properties.

Atomic weight: 266
Melting point: unknown

#110

Ununnilium

Uun

Discovery: Peter Armbruster in 1994

Origin of name: The element has not yet been given an official name. Its temporary name is derived from its atomic number.

Fewer than half a dozen atoms of ununnilium have been created by bombarding lead with atoms of nickel. With a half-life only half a thousandth of a second, little is known about the properties of the element.

Atomic weight: 269
Melting point: unknown

NAMING THE ELEMENTS

Until the early 1990s, the privilege of naming a new element had always belonged to the discoverer. This presented few difficulties when elements were being discovered by lone researchers or, at best, small teams of scientists. However, as the twentieth century progressed and research into the creation of new elements became increasingly complex, the search for new elements was being conducted in many countries simultaneously, and by very large teams of scientists. This naturally led to disputes on who was the first to make a discovery and, of course, who had the right to name the new element. To resolve such disputes, a special commission was created by the International Union of Pure and Applied Chemists. This commission votes on the suitability of the name proposed for a new element (the name seaborgium was originally disallowed because Glenn Seaborg was still alive) and, in fact, suggested temporary names in advance for yet-to-be-discovered elements 104, 105, 106, 107, and 108. These temporary names are based on the Latin words for their numbers:

0 = nil	**5 = pent**
1 = un	**6 = hex**
2 = bi	**7 = sept**
3 = tri	**8 = oct**
4 = quad	**9 = enn**

According to this system, element 112 would be called ununbiium—1-1-2—until a permanent name is officially designated.

Many of the elements had names proposed for them that were never accepted, just as there have been names suggested for elements that later proved to be nonexistent. You will look in vain, then, for elements such as crodonium, emanation, alabamine, angularium, paradoxium, cyclonium, demonium, exactinio, offium, phtor, and ptene (which is probably just as well).

#111

Unununium
Uuu

Discovery: A team of scientists at the Gesellschaft für Schwerionenforshung in Germany in 1994

Origin of name: The element has not yet been given an official name. Its temporary name is derived from its atomic number.

Only three atoms of unununium have been created, by bombarding bismuth with atoms of nickel. Little is known about the chemical properties of unununium because of its half-life of only four thousandths of a second.

Atomic weight: 272
Melting point: unknown

#112

Ununbiium
Uub

Discovery: A team of scientists at the Gesellschaft für Schwerionenforshung in Germany in 1996

Origin of name: The element has not yet been given an official name. Its temporary name is derived from its atomic number.

Ununbiium is created by bombarding lead with atoms of zinc. Only a few atoms of the element have ever been created, and little is known about its properties.

Atomic weight: 277
Melting point: unknown

#113

Unknown

#114

Ununquadium
Uuq

Discovery: A team of scientists at the Joint Institute for Nuclear Research in Russia in 1999

Origin of name: The element has not yet been given an official name. Its temporary name is derived from its atomic number.

Although only a few atoms of ununquadium have been created, it has a much longer half-life—between 30 seconds and 11 minutes, depending on the isotope—than elements such as ununbiium and others. This increase in longevity has led some scientists to predict the existence of a region of stability—a region where long-lived elements might be found—among the otherwise short-lived superheavy elements. These elements would be much easier to study and work with. Ununquadium is created by bombarding plutonium with calcium nuclei. After forty days a single atom of ununquadium was produced.

Atomic weight: 285
Melting point: unknown

Beyond #114?

Scientists are still searching for new elements. There are still gaps to be filled in the periodic table—a missing element between elements 112 and 114, for instance, and whatever may lie beyond ununquadium. In 1999 a team of scientists at the Lawrence Berkeley National Laboratory in California announced that they had created element #118, ununoctium, the heaviest member of the periodic table so far found, during high-energy impacts inside a particle accelerator. The scientists believed that ununoctium decayed rapidly into other elements, including never-before-seen element #116. (Since then, the Joint Institute for Nuclear Research in Dubna, Russia, appears to have created element 116, ununhexium, directly.) "It's tough when an element disappears," the director of the laboratory said in retracting the original announcement.

The Lore of the Elements

Actinide Series: the chemical elements that lie between actinium and nobelium in the periodic table

alchemy: an ancient pseudoscience that eventually evolved into the science of chemistry

alkali metals: the elements in group 1 of the periodic table—lithium, sodium, potassium, rubidium, cesium, and francium. They are all highly reactive metals.

allotrope: one of two or more distinctly different forms of an element

alloy: a combination of two or more metals

alpha particle: a particle emitted by radioactive substances; it consists of two neutrons and two protons—basically identical to the nucleus of a helium atom

alpha ray: a stream of alpha particles

alum: a compound composed of sulfur and one of the alkali metals

amalgam: any alloy containing mercury

anode: the negative pole in a vacuum tube

atom: the smallest unit of an element

atomic number: the number of protons in the nucleus of an element's atom

atomic weight: the average weight of the isotopes of an element

beta particle: a fast-moving electron or positron ejected from an atom during beta decay

beta ray: a stream of beta particles emitted by a radioactive substance

carcinogen: a substance that encourages or causes cancer to grow

catalyst: a substance that initiates or sustains a chemical reaction without taking part in it itself

cathode: the positive pole in a vacuum tube

cathode ray: a beam of high-speed electrons emitted by a cathode; they light up the screen of a cathode ray tube, such as a computer's monitor

compound: a chemical combination of two or more elements

cyclotron: a machine that uses powerful magnets to accelerate atomic particles to tremendous speeds

decay: the process in which the nucleus of a radioactive element breaks up, forming a new element

deuteron: the nucleus of a deuterium atom, consisting of one proton and one neutron

electrolysis: the process by which an electrical current is used to break a compound into its component elements

electron: a basic particle found in the atom; it has a negative electrical charge

element: a substance that cannot be reduced to a simpler substance

fission: the splitting of an object (such as the nucleus of an atom) into two or more fragments

fluorocarbon: a compound in which the molecules contain both fluorine and carbon

gamma ray: a powerful form of radiation emitted by radioactive substances; it is part of the electromagnetic spectrum

gild: to coat an object with a thin layer of gold

gluons: subatomic particles responsible for the force that holds quarks together so they can form protons and neutrons

group: the elements that make up one or more vertical columns in the periodic table

hadron: a subatomic particle composed of quarks and gluons

half-life: the time required for half of a radioactive substance to decay

halogen: one of the elements in group 17 of the periodic table—fluorine, chlorine, bromine, iodine, and astatine. The word means "salt former" since these elements create salts when combined with other elements.

inert: the inability to combine with other elements or compounds

isotopes: atoms of an element that contain the same number of protons but different numbers of neutrons; different isotopes of an element may have different chemical properties

Lanthanide Series: the Rare Earth elements that lie between lanthanum and ytterbium in the periodic table

lepton: a subatomic particle that is not made of quarks, such as the electron

light-emitting diode (LED): a device that takes advantage of the fact that some substances, such as gallium arsenide, can turn electricity directly into light

molecule: a combination of two or more atoms

neutron: a basic particle found in the nucleus of an atom; it has no electrical charge

nuclear fission: the process by which the nucleus of an atom is split into separate particles or groups of particles

nucleus: the core of an atom, which is composed of protons and neutrons

oxidize: to combine with oxygen

ozone: a molecule consisting of three atoms of oxygen; at normal temperatures and pressures, it is a blue gas

period: a horizontal row in the periodic table

periodic table: a list of the chemical elements, arranged by electron structure so that elements with related chemical properties form a regular, or periodic, series

phosphors: the light-emitting substances on the surface of a television screen

photoconductive: the quality of being an electrical conductor when exposed to light

photosynthesis: the process by which many plants produce food using the energy of sunlight

photovoltaic: the process by which electricity is produced from light

proton: a basic particle found in the nucleus of an atom; it has a positive electrical charge

pseudoscience: a "science" that is based on superstition or false premises

quark: the smallest subatomic particle, believed to be one of the fundamental building blocks of matter

radioactivity: the process during which a substance gives off, or radiates, atomic particles

reactive: the property of combining readily with other elements and compounds

semiconductor: a material with an electrical conductance halfway between conductors and non-conductors

solder: a low-melting-point alloy used to make connections in electronic equipment and by plumbers to connect and seal metal pipes

spectrum: the colored band of light created when white light is passed through a prism

subatomic: describes particles smaller than atoms

sublime: to turn directly from solid form into a gas, without first passing through a liquid phase superconductor: a substance that offers little or no resistance to an electric current

transition elements: the thirty-eight elements in groups 3 through 12 in the periodic table; they are all metals with high tensile strength, density, and melting points.

transmutation: the changing of one element into another

transuranium elements: the elements that follow uranium in the periodic table

X-ray: a short wavelength radiation that has a high power of penetration

Further Reading

Levi, Primo. *The Periodic Table*. New York: Random House, 1996.

Quinn, Susan. *Marie Curie: A Life*. New York: Simon & Schuster, 1995.

Strathem, Paul. *Mendeleyev's Dream: The Quest for the Elements*. New York: St. Martin's, 2001.

Stwertka, Albert. *A Guide to the Elements*. New York: Oxford University Press, 2002.

Web Sites

The Element Collection
http://www.theodoregray.com/PeriodicTable/index.html
A fun site with lots of information about how the reader can create his or her own collection of elements

The Visual Elements
www.chemsoc.org/viselements/
A visually beautiful tour through the periodic table conducted by the Royal Society of Chemistry

Elementymology
www.vanderkrogt.net/elements/
A highly detailed site devoted to the discovery of each of the elements and the history of their names

WebElements Periodic Table
www.webelements.com/
The most complete guide on the Web to the periodic table and the elements

Index

Page numbers in *italics* refer to illustrations.

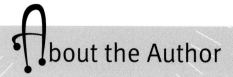

About the Author

Hugo Award-winner Ron Miller is an illustrator and author who specializes in astronomy. He has created or contributed to many books on the subject, including *Cycles of Fire, The History of Earth,* and *The Grand Tour.* Among his nonfiction books for young people are *The History of Rockets* and *The History of Science Fiction,* as well as the Worlds Beyond series, which won the 2003 American Institute of Physics Science Writing Award in Physics and Astronomy. Miller's work has won many other awards and distinctions, including the 2002 Hugo Award for Best Non-Fiction for *The Art of Chesley Bonestell.* He has designed a set of ten commemorative stamps on the planets in our solar system for the U.S. Postal Service. He has written several novels and has worked on a number of science-fiction films, such as *Dune* and *Total Recall.* His original paintings can be found in collections all over the world, including that of the National Air and Space Museum in Washington, D.C., and magazines such as *National Geographic, Scientific American, Sky and Telescope,* and *Natural History.* Miller lives in King George, Virginia, with his wife and cats.